# SECRET
## EXECUTIONERS

# THE
# SECRET
# EXECUTIONERS

### THE AMAZING TRUE STORY OF THE DEATH SQUAD THAT TRACKED DOWN AND KILLED NAZI WAR CRIMINALS

## DANNY BAZ

JOHN BLAKE

Published by John Blake Publishing Ltd,
3 Bramber Court, 2 Bramber Road,
London W14 9PB, England

www.johnblakepublishing.co.uk

First published in paperback in 2007
by Grasset as Ni Oubli Ni Pardon
UK hardback edition published 2009 by John Blake Publishing Ltd
translated by Catherine Spencer
This paperback edition published 2010

ISBN: 978 1 84454 952 8

British Library Cataloguing-in-Publication Data:

A catalogue record for this book is available from the British Library.

Design by www.envydesign.co.uk

Printed in Great Britain by CPI Bookmarque, Croydon CRO 4TD

1 3 5 7 9 10 8 6 4 2

Papers used by John Blake Publishing are natural, recyclable products made
from wood grown in sustainable forests. The manufacturing processes conform
to the environmental regulations of the country of origin.

*I dedicate this book to all those I love:*

To my beloved family.
To my parents: Max, may his memory be blessed,
and Bianca, may she enjoy long life.
To my friend Giora.
To members of 'The Owl', John and Roger,
and all our friends.
To the memory of the innocent children massacred
during the Holocaust –

'We will never forget! We will never forgive!'


*I particularly wish to thank:*

Special thanks to the late Naomi Frenkel.
The late, lamented Ted Arison.
Mickey and Allan Davis of Chicago.
The Israeli Defence Minister.
The wounded war veterans' association of the
Israeli Defence Ministry.

Resistance also consists of the action of those Jewish doctors who refuse to sign the certificates of 'death from contagious illness' of those gypsies who have just been gassed. It is those women who, arriving from Warsaw in October 1944, threw themselves on the SS before they perished. It is that Jewish woman who, before going into the 'Bunker', cried out to the SS: 'Our brothers in the world will not rest until they have taken revenge in the name of our innocent blood.'

*Georges Bensoussan, in* Des voix sous la cendre, *Shoah Memorial / Calmann-Lévy, Paris, 2005.*

# MOST WANTED

We are seeking — for a reward
of 130,000 euros:
Dr ARIBERT HEIM

Born 28/06/1914 in Radkersburg,
Austria
Height: 1.90 m.
Colour of eyes: Dark blue-grey
Powerful, athletic appearance
Upside down V-shaped scar to
right of mouth
Shoe size: 47

Dr Aribert Heim is suspected of having assassinated
numerous prisoners by injection into the heart when
he was the SS doctor in Mauthausen concentration camp.

He is being sought under an international warrant
issued by the court of the Land of Baden-Baden.

A reward of 130,000 euros is offered in exchange
for information leading to the arrest of the wanted
man. This reward is exclusively reserved for private
individuals and excludes officials whose work
involves the pursuit of those guilty of punishable
offences.

Please transmit all information to the
crime police of the Land of Bade-Wurtemberg,
tel. 0711/5401-xxxx, to any other police service,
or by e-mail: flz ka.bwl.de

# PROLOGUE

## 'May the beast die!'

ARIBERT HEIM IS THE LAST NAZI WAR CRIMINAL STILL ACTIVELY SOUGHT THROUGHOUT THE ENTIRE WORLD. Not only by the German police; the Spanish, Chilean, Argentinean and Uruguayan authorities are also on the lookout for him. He is the number one target of the Nazi-hunting organisation founded by Simon Wiesenthal. In recent years, he has been spotted in Germany, Egypt, Spain and Latin America.

Aribert Heim is, however, dead.

I took part in the operation that led to his execution in 1982.

*

The two photos of Heim displayed on the website of the Bade-Wurtemberg police, under the caption 'Most Wanted', are the only two that exist of him. The first was taken in 1950, the second nine years later. They show a handsome man, a former ice-hockey player, in the prime of life – confident of himself and of his charm. When I look at them, I cannot help thinking of another image of Aribert Heim, one which no one will ever see. That of a man who had lost his arrogant pride: we had just captured him and his fate was sealed; he was wounded, tired and anxious. His expression will haunt me until the end of my days. Even monsters die.

This book recounts the tracking and capture of the man, nicknamed 'Dr Death' by the deportees of Mauthausen camp, by a secret organisation that was active throughout the 1980s and which had the mission of unmasking and eliminating Nazi war criminals who were clandestine refugees in North or South America.

Christened 'The Owl', it was created by survivors of the Holocaust who belonged to wealthy families and who were well known in business circles, and benefited, behind the scenes, from widespread and powerful support. Its members led a double life. While keeping up the façade of respectable businessmen, they waged a secret and ruthless war, single-mindedly tracking down Nazi war criminals who believed they were safe from human judgement. This organisation of avengers had judged and executed the members of 'Shock Squadron 5' that had, under the leadership of Zobrach, Namsila and Lichtanker, massacred dozens of thousands of Balkan Jews, including some of the relations of the founders of

# PROLOGUE

The Owl. Other particularly bloody Nazi brutes, members of the Fascist group of the Arrow Cross Party which reigned in Hungary during the war, paid for their crimes by meeting with the same fate.

All the members of The Owl were Jewish. Many of them had survived the Holocaust, or were the sons or grandsons of survivors; some of them occupied senior posts at the heart of the American administration, in various security organisations (the FBI and the CIA) or in the Department of Justice. Others were former members of the special services. Driven by a fierce desire for revenge, they did not hesitate to risk all they had, their family and their goods, to arrest and execute one of the last great Nazi war criminals still at large.

I am proud of having taken part in this relentless hunt, which lasted almost two years and which has never been recounted. Some of my comrades would have preferred me to keep silent while others encouraged me to tell the truth about the end of Aribert Heim. The names of my companions in arms have been disguised, in order not to break the confidentiality of our organisation, which benefited from a limitless budget, worthy of the largest secret services. This book recounts facts that are rigorously true. However, for reasons of confidentiality, certain episodes have deliberately been omitted.

'Remember, do not forgive, pursue step by step.' That was the command given by The Owl and it perfectly sums up its character and mission. At the end of the 1980s, having achieved most of its goals and, above all, fearing that its existence would eventually be exposed, it decided to put an end to its activities.

*

Like all my comrades, I was experienced in the techniques of secret warfare. I had taken part in the Yom Kippur war, as a captain. When I entered The Owl, I had the rank of captain in the Israeli air force. I had carried out several missions in Africa, the United States and France. At the beginning of the 1990s, I assisted in the training of special units of the Ethiopian army of Mengistu, whose mission was to save Ethiopian Jews and repatriate them to Israel. I had also led training courses for foreign officers at Mitzpe Ramon, under a remit of inter-national co-operation, among whom were American officers newly graduated from the military academies of West Point, Carlyle and Colorado Springs. I had also carried out missions in the Congo, at the time of Mobutu. My African experiences were the subject of an article ('African Connection') on the military and civilian co-operation between Israel and Africa, which had a certain impact in Israel. As did my first book, in which I gave a fictionalised account of the hunt for Aribert Heim – without revealing the name of our quarry or my role in the chase.

Why have I now decided to recount this untold story? Firstly, for my children. Several years ago, my daughter was preparing to leave on a school trip to Auschwitz. Before she left, our family watched a documentary on the Holocaust. By the end of it, she was overcome with emotion. Seeing her tears, I said to myself that I owed it to her to tell my story. So that she would know that men had once risen up against forgetting and forgiveness. I wanted my children to be proud of what we did.

\*

Today, his widow and one of his sons still live in the house of Aribert Heim in Baden-Baden. The public prosecutor of Baden-Baden, Mikaël Kloze, has interrogated the old lady, described in a press article as 'good-mannered, if a touch strait-laced'. When the procurer showed her documents referring to these monstrous crimes, she gave a hand gesture as if she were chasing away a fly, a bad thought or a burdensome memory. And she repeated: 'I didn't know.'[1]

Journalists chasing scoops and Nazis regularly turn up in Baden-Baden in the hope of restarting the hunt for Aribert Heim. On the website of the French TV channel France 3, the programme *Pièces à conviction* can be watched; first broadcast in December 2005, it dealt with the 'last hunt' for Nazi war criminals. 'Simon Wiesenthal died at the age of 96 in Vienna on 20 September 2005,' explained the makers of the programme. 'But the work of the greatest Nazi hunter has not ended with

1 Marie-France Etchegoin and Annette Gerlach: *The search for the 'butcher of Mauthausen'*, *Le Nouvel Observateur*, 20 October 2005.

him. The foundation bearing his name has just launched a huge programme to track down the last dignitaries of the Hitler regime. Its name: "Operation Last Chance". It is this last manhunt that the cameras of *Pièces à conviction* have followed all over Europe and even to Jerusalem. "Last", because its chances of success diminish with time. There are fewer and fewer former Nazis, brought down by time and old age if not by human justice. The hunters have to take part in a veritable race against the clock. The last trail to date: the reappearance of Dr Aribert Heim in Spain. A Nazi who must be caught quickly: today, he would be 91 years old...'

Aribert Heim is in good company. The programme compared the hunt for him to that for Aloïs Brunner, hiding out in Syria, and Klaus Barbie, tracked down in Bolivia. It referred to Adolf Eichmann's kidnapping in Argentina by the Israeli secret services, which resulted in his trial and execution. However, the journalists on the programme were unaware that another avenging organisation replaced the Israeli secret services who, after Eichmann was taken, gave up tracking down the remaining Nazi war criminals.

As I watched the images of Aribert Heim's house in Baden-Baden again on France 3, I thought of my long hours of secret surveillance carried out in the company of a senior CIA agent, completely devoted to our cause, and two of his men. I saw us tailing Frieda Heim and her children to make sure that Dr Death had not returned to the superb house in which he had lived and practised until 1962...

# PROLOGUE

Forty-five years of being on the run make Aribert Heim a serious candidate for the record books and there is no reason why the hunt should end as long as no one has blown the whistle on it. Which is why police, Nazi trackers and journalists were still continuing, in 2007, to pursue an old man who would have celebrated his 93rd birthday last June – if we had not executed him more than a quarter of a century ago.

*

At the end of the Second World War, the Americans rounded up tens of thousands of former Nazis. They placed General Gehlen, who had formerly run Hitler's Soviet Union intelligence services, at the head of a secret anti-Communist organisation – the ancestor of the West German secret services (the BND). The Americans did not want to acknowledge that the Gehlen organisation harboured hundreds of former SS. With the support of the American army, and then of the heads of the CIA, General Gehlen was able to build his organisation by drawing from the Nazi pool.

At that period, Aribert Heim was one of the prominent figures of Baden-Baden. Married to Frieda Berthold, the daughter of a notable family of the region, he opened a health centre, frequented by the upper crust of the town. But everything changed in 1960, after Adolf Eichmann was captured in Argentina. The worlds of Aribert Heim and his kind collapsed. Germans and Americans alike realised that thousands of war criminals had never been tried. The Germans reopened old wounds, at least superficially, and dozens of Nazis were brought before the courts. Including Aribert Heim. But a guardian angel was watching over Dr Death: just before he was due to be arrested, he hastily left home, after receiving a phone call from a friend in high places (we will never know who) informing him that the police were on their way to arrest him.

For years, the Americans denied having had contact with any Nazi criminals or organisations. But a commission of inquiry set up by Congress in 1977 revealed that tens of thousands of Nazi war criminals and their auxiliaries had found refuge in the United States, where they had been living for years in the most total secrecy and relative tranquillity. The scandal was such that the government created a special organisation (the OSI) that was charged with finding these people who had entered American territory illegally. More than a hundred war criminals were then expelled; in 2007, the OSI was still looking for over two hundred more.

In 1998, President Clinton signed the Nazi War Disclosure Act, ordering all government agencies to declassify most of their documents concerning former Nazis. The operation was overseen by a special commission, the Nazi War Crimes Interagency Working Group (IWG), which brought together senior officials from the main American secret services (the CIA and the NSA), counter-espionage (the FBI) and the Pentagon. The IWG made public almost eight million pages of documents that had been classified top secret – some of which had been communicated to The Owl by our sources.

*

Questioned by *Le Nouvel Observateur* in 2005, the German policeman responsible for the Heim case declared, 'He is alive.' The magazine explained: 'The man who states this is in his fifties and has a calm, paternal air. He has been working on the case full-time for more than a year, with the support of his hierarchy who want to bring it to a successful conclusion. Very recently he has reopened a trail: that of the bank accounts. "Heim, a good Nazi and a good organiser, amassed money before escaping," he explains. "Today, in a Berliner Sparkasse account in his name, there are almost a million euros. As well as a portfolio of shares."'

Dr Death indeed enjoyed impressive wealth. As I will describe, during our first raid on Aribert Heim and his men, we seized a briefcase containing diamonds and documents concerning some of the treasures hidden by the Nazis in Alpine lakes in 1945. Heim was a rich man, a very rich man, who in addition to his official revenues managed a fortune inherited from the Third Reich. Money is at the heart of the Aribert Heim mystery. This clandestine fortune is doubtless at the origin of the silence that continues to weigh around his death, even if it prevents the family from claiming their rightful inheritance. The lawyer looking after the interests of the Heim family continues to request, every year, a tax exemption on his client's revenues, on the basis that he is 'resident abroad'. The police responsible for tracking down Aribert Heim talk about 'very convincing clues that have recently been found'. Following the trail of Dr Death's official income, they came across his sister Herta who, in the 1970s, was collecting the rents of the Berlin building of which he was the landlord.

By capturing Aribert Heim, we uncovered part of the mystery surrounding his disappearance. For mainly financial reasons, therefore, a powerful organisation took pains – and continues to do so – to cover up his traces and to make out that he is still alive – particularly by use of doubles. He was spotted in Egypt, working for Nasser's police, between 1963 and 1967. He is said to be in Paysandu, Uruguay, near the border with Argentina, in a sanctuary for former SS, brought there via various channels such as the 'Rat Line' or 'Odessa'. In 1985 (that is, three years after his execution), the Stuttgart police received information that it believed reliable: the Nazi had taken refuge somewhere deep in the Amazon jungle. An inspector rushed off to interrogate a half-mad old man who didn't even look like Aribert Heim... Then the German police took off to Argentina. With no more success. The hunt continued at the start of the 21st century, this time in Spain. Dr Death was said to have been seen on the island of Ibiza, in a colony of former SS in Figueral. From time to time, his trackers intercepted postcards addressed to his family in Baden-Baden: *'Es geht mir gut'* ('I am well')... The German police were alerted by strange transfers of funds: 220,000 dollars had left Heim's account in the Berlin bank and ended up in that of an artist couple in Ibiza. Now, the day of the transfer, the two artists were in Denmark, where they picked up a parking ticket in Copenhagen... not far from an office rented by one of Aribert Heim's sons! All this showed that someone was clearly trying to lay a false trail. In April 2006, the chase again changed venue, once again to Latin America. The court of Baden-Baden issued a new international arrest warrant. The German authorities re-examined the Uruguayan trail and then turned, following more 'convincing clues', towards Chile. All of which was, needless to say, in vain.

And so, the legend of an Aribert Heim who is still alive and uncapturable persists, fed by powerful networks that have covered up his disappearance – they cannot announce the death of their protégé without revealing their own existence and overturning considerable economic interests.

This legend now comes to an end. The Butcher of Mauthausen was not in Spain, or Uruguay, or Germany, or Argentina... He was in the United States. Where, 25 years ago, we hunted him down, captured him, judged and then executed him. This book tells how.

# CHAPTER 1
# THE RECRUIT

THAT SUMMER OF 1980, NEW YORK LAY SWELTERING UNDER A BAND OF HEAT. The traffic jams were more interminable than ever: it took two and a half hours to get from Kennedy airport to the small, well-kept house in Brooklyn – my favourite area of New York – where I had found, more than friends, a real family. I spent most of my time there. A deep friendship was forged with these people during long nocturnal conversations: their history, like mine, had been marked for ever by the Holocaust. I had been brought up on horror stories: cattle trucks bearing all my grandfather's family to their death and the atrocities committed by the Nazis...

That evening, like every Friday evening, we were standing around the table. The head of the house had lit the candles.

1

Wine and herbs were in the middle of the table. I felt good in this very religious atmosphere, in the heart of Brooklyn. These are such simple people. I knew only two or three of the guests. During the meal we talked, as usual, about Israel, the Holocaust, the victims, the monsters...

'I don't understand how thousands of Nazis are living peacefully all over the world with impunity. They are even here in the United States! Do you know that since the 1950s almost 100,000 have come here, and no one does anything!'

I did not know. I shared the indignation of the head of the house and I wished I could do something to avenge all these innocents, all these victims of the Nazi madness...

At the other end of the table, a man was following the conversation in silence. A flamboyant man in his sixties with a dangerous, wolf-like face and white hair cut short, he had the confidence of those who have been successful in life. His azure blue almond-shaped eyes were staring at me. He then pronounced, for my benefit:

'We'll talk more about that later.'

The conversation had already jumped on to other topics.

'We'll talk more about it later.' Throughout the meal, that little phrase obsessed me.

After dinner, in the sitting room, the man with the wolf-like face came up to me and introduced himself:

'Ted Arison.'

This millionaire, one of the pioneers of the cruise industry, had created Carnival Cruise in 1972, which rapidly became the leading presence on the world sea cruise market with more than 3 million passengers a year. Arison formed part of Pal'mach, the first special Israeli force units operating under British control. I am today giving his real name because he has died.

He showed interest in my service history — I got the impression that he already knew all about it.

'You were a bomber fighter pilot, is that right?'

'Oh, you know, before coming here I did a lot of things. I was part of the frogman commando of the Israeli Marines. When I'd had enough of that, I joined the air force. That was unheard of! A marine joining the air force camp!'

'Yes, I can imagine… And why did you accept this job at JFK?'

'For the challenge. It was something new for me. In the beginning, I found it interesting. Testing the security of El Al cargo flights. Then I confess the work started to weigh on me. What happened to our friends was the straw that broke the camel's back. You know, the relative they have just lost was put in a coffin by a rabbi in a religious ceremony at the synagogue. The coffin was to be sent to Jerusalem and those idiots at El Al demanded that it be opened and searched, to make sure it did not contain gold or jewellery… or weapons! It's ridiculous! Why pile suffering on suffering? You only have to see them to understand what kind of people they are. I intervened and opposed that decision. I won out, and that didn't go down well. The severe criticism I made resulted in my being marginalised. They want to get rid of me, but I don't regret doing what I did. All of which is to say... that I think I miss action!'

'In any case, our hosts this evening seem to like you very much,' he said.

It was strange. I had the curious impression that this man was putting me through an important exam, that he was testing and evaluating me. Captivated by the warmth of the welcome and the kindness of these people who all seem to know each other, I agreed to play the game. And then I wanted to know exactly what he meant by that little phrase: 'We'll talk more about it later.' More than 20 years have passed and I still wonder whether that meal had not been organised to enable that job interview to take place.

I turned the conversation to the Holocaust.

'You know, Ted, I think that everyone here is a victim or the son of a victim of the Nazi barbarity. I will never forget all the stories that my grandfather and my mother told me, all that horror...'

'Your grandfather... He survived?'

'Of his whole family, three escaped. My grandfather and his two children, his son and daughter – my mother. She was never able to forget the piercing shrieking of the Stuka bomber planes. Years later, she told me about her terror when she heard the noise of my fighter plane engine as I passed over her house in Haifa... She spent the war in hiding in a small Rumanian village. Her father, my grandfather, was not as fortunate and he was arrested and transported, crammed with dozens of others in a cattle truck. The Germans did not give them either water or food. He told me he had seen people drinking others' urine they were so thirsty. People suffocated in the cattle truck; my grandfather had been able to breathe through two uneven planks. At the end of the journey, they were all dead except him.'

Ted Arison stared at me. After a long silence, he said:

'You speak about avenging the victims of the Holocaust... You know that the beasts have never paid for their crimes. For every Eichmann, who was tried and hanged in Jerusalem, how many Mengeles are still alive? Some of them live a stone's throw from here. In this country, the United States, there are thousands, perhaps tens of thousands, of former Nazis living peacefully! It's an intolerable situation.'

'I don't understand. Why has nothing been done since Eichmann?'

He shot a glance at me, with his insistent blue eyes, smiling slightly:

'Who told you that nothing has been done? What if I told you that, behind the scenes, friends are acting to avenge the victims of the Holocaust?'

At which point I threw out in reply, sealing my fate:

'How can I join them?'

\*

A month later, a telephone call.

'Danny? I am phoning you on behalf of our friend.'

My heart started racing. I had been waiting for this call for weeks. Since Ted Arison allowed me a glimpse of a secret organisation, I had been living only for this moment. I had thought about that evening dozens of time, and about my conversation with Ted, analysing the silences, the unspoken words, asking myself again and again the single question: how can I join the avengers?

The man on the phone introduced himself as John. I agreed to meet him in a café in Queens, the 'Q Garden'. He was a tall fellow, impressive and charismatic – and very funny, with a strong predilection for swear words. Africa, Vietnam: he had been in all the secret wars. For years he had been working for the CIA, currently in the headquarters at Langley, and was a senior official of 'the Agency'. In this capacity, he was one of the avengers' organisation's most precious recruits. A pro. And like all former soldiers of his age, he talked about Vietnam without my being able to work out what organisation he had belonged to at the time – it wasn't the CIA, which he joined later. Perhaps the Green Berets... I would later learn that his unit specialised in suicide missions such as tracking the Vietcong in tunnels dug out under the jungle or penetrating enemy towns through the drains.

For the next two hours, John tested me. He wanted to know who I was, what I thought, what I had done; he wanted to understand my motivation and make sure that my intentions were serious. We swapped military experiences. He gave me to understand that he belonged to an organisation. When he told me that he was interested in the issue of revenge, I mistakenly deduced that he was trying to set up a new organisation, for which he was seeking volunteers. In fact, John was already part of a secret group that had the mission of bringing to justice and punishing SS war criminals living in North America. The guilt of these criminals had been irrefutably proved – by, among other things, documents issuing from governmental sources in the United States and Europe.

I did not know how long this highly structured and compartmentalised organisation had been operating in the United States. Ten, perhaps twenty years? Had it already eliminated Nazi war criminals? How many? A mystery. Its members were intelligence officers, federal agents of the FBI, senior officials of the Department of Justice or else former policemen. These men had all lost confidence in their country's judicial system when it came to punishing the former Nazis. They could no longer accept the evasions and diversions. They believed that the Office of Special Investigations (OSI), the branch of the Department of Justice responsible for tracking down the Nazis, had not done enough. Almost all these war criminals had entered the United States illegally and obtained American nationality by making false declarations. The main mission of the OSI was to bring them before federal courts to strip them of their American nationality and send them back to their native country.

Acting principally from California, the members of this group had numerous contacts and close links with governmental institutions, particularly the FBI and the CIA. The department for immigration and above all the Department of Justice in the United States had the most sordid state secrets in their archives. They knew about the presence on American soil of the Nazis, some of whom had obtained the status of legal residents. This intelligence formed the basis of the plan to capture and punish these criminals. Additional information was provided by sources linked to the Director of Public Prosecutions in Germany and in Poland, the latter having access to certain documents contained in the KGB archives.

'If they offer you something, you should resign from your current post,' John forewarned me.

I wanted to say to him: 'If you make me the offer I'm thinking about, I would resign on the spot to join you.' But something held me back. I needed to know more.

I left John in a state of excitement that would never leave me. My military past made me the ideal recruit. The idea of taking part in secret operations against the Nazis filled me with indescribable excitement and pride. I thought with emotion of all those children massacred during the Holocaust; I felt ready to do anything in order to have the honour of avenging them. My existence took on a new meaning and a new goal, a little as if I had had a divine revelation. Nothing upset me, not even the fact that I still knew nothing about the operations or risks in question.

Two weeks later, there was another call and another rendezvous; same time, same place. This time, the man from the CIA had not come alone. He was accompanied by a man in his sixties – let's call him 'Barney'. John seemed transported, resembling a little boy sitting obediently beside his father. I had the clear impression, which was afterwards confirmed, that Barney was in fact the head of the entire operation. He began speaking:

'Danny, I've made my fortune in Texas and I am ready to spend everything I have earned, to my last dollar, to see the Nazis who have taken refuge in the United States finally paying for their crimes.'

He confirmed that a secret organisation existed. The talk was no longer of a project but of an operation already under way, completely up and running, in which he planned to invest six million dollars.

'Six million dollars to avenge the six million deaths of the Holocaust. And if it is not enough, I will add to it.'

'How do you operate? You find the targets then eliminate them?'

'We are an organisation of avengers and we do what the justice system in North and South America refuses to do. We have gathered all we need in terms of proof and documents. We have contacts in high places. Our organisation is totally compartmentalised. Those responsible choose a target. A first team begins the hunt. Its mission is at that time to seize the target with as little bloodshed as possible.'

'So it's a military operation...'

'Yes, in a sense… If we have to kill, we kill. If we can avoid it, we avoid it.'

'So you capture your target. And afterwards?'

'The first team seizes our man, then hand him over to a second team who take him before a tribunal made up of Holocaust survivors.'

'Why a tribunal? Isn't the verdict already known in advance?'

'Yes, of course. But we want the rats to face their victims before they die. What do you say?'

I needed a little time to reflect.

'Take your time. You can join us when you want. Let us know as soon as you are ready. You will always have a place among us.'

*

Tel Aviv, several months later. It was a hot and humid evening. In the familiar hubbub of Ben Gurion airport, I was late and, under the amused gaze of a couple of travelers, I hurried towards the El Al check-in desk, my large suitcase wobbling dangerously on its half-broken wheels.

Before take off, I got out of my pocket the text of the prayer that I usually recite before each trip I took. This time, however, I murmur the words with particular fervour. I am going to need divine protection more than ever.

After a short wait on the runway, the vibrations of the plane intensified. Fifty seconds later, we were on our way to New York. The Israeli coast disappeared, leaving behind my house, my family and friends. I was single, without children or ties, and ready for adventure.

This trip was going to plunge me into the most incredible of manhunts. It began in the superb property in Queens where I turned up two hours after having landed at JFK airport in New York. It was an imposing building; in the middle was an entrance mounted by a central porthole surrounded by little windows. The sloping roofs overhung enormous bay windows. The whole thing emanated an impression of luxurious harmony. Two flights of steps separated by a long corridor led to a solid wooden door painted in white. I played with the keys to the house. I felt good here, at home, and I knew that once I was inside the door, my life was going to be overturned. Without hesitation, I went into the house, after having disconnected the alarm system, and left my luggage in the hall at the foot of the stairway. On an occasional table was a telephone. I dialled a number in California.

'I got here safely.'

On the other end of the line, Barney's joyful voice rang out:

'Welcome, Danny! I hope you had no trouble collecting the keys. Settle in wherever you like. We'll be back at the end of the week.'

'I'm looking forward to seeing you. But I should have gone to a hotel – it's too beautiful here...'

'Danny, when you phoned me from Israel to tell me you

were coming, what did I say to you? You are at home here, you stay as long as you want and come back whenever you want.'

'I know… I don't know how to thank you.'

After a long silence, I blurted out:

'Listen, Barney, I have something important to say to you… I would be very happy to help you get rid of the rats that are swarming in the yard…'

Silence. This time, it was the other man who was searching for the right words.

'We knew we could count on you. We are very proud to have you among us.'

*Rats*, that is what our organisation called the Nazis living in the United States. I say 'our' because from the moment of this phone call, I had given everything up to join this secret group, christened, in honour of one of the rat's predators, 'The Owl'.

I settled myself in luxurious comfort in an armchair in front of the sitting room television and attempted to watch the news. Shattered by the journey, I slipped into a deep sleep – to be woken by hunger and thirst twelve hours later. I dragged myself to the kitchen. I was going to need a strong coffee to get back on my feet. Cup in hand, I made for the swimming pool, in the garden filled with flowers and plants; the turquoise water was irresistible and in a split second, I had taken off my clothes, dived in and forgotten everything as I swam serenely, a sense of excitement nonetheless bubbling inside. On my fortieth length, the phone rang. Barney.

'Hi, Danny! Did you sleep well? Listen, we've decided to come back earlier than planned. We'll be there in two days' time. We intend to spend some holiday time at Hunter Mountain, three hours' drive from New York. There'll be several other friends there, it'll be a valuable time...'

Something is obviously being planned.... A thousand questions flooded into my mind but this was something that could not be dealt with on the phone. Patience.

I took advantage of the two days left before my friends returned to study the topography of Hunter Mountain and its surroundings by charting the position of the streams, gorges and pathways, making a systematic analysis worthy of a military chief of staff – like a navigator carefully studying his roadmap...

Barney and his companions returned from California in the afternoon. We greeted each other warmly. After the hugs, everyone sat down around a light snack. I felt at ease among these people; I already had the impression that I belonged to their family.

Barney suddenly asks me, out of the blue:

'Danny, are you sure of your decision? Once you're with us, it's impossible to go into reverse. You won't be able to speak to your family or your friends for a long time.'

'I am here, Barney.'

He then handed me a thick file marked 'TOP SECRET'. It contained photocopies of documents, most of them in English, taken from files in the secret archives of the CIA, the

FBI or the Department of Justice. Certain pages were in German. On these I noticed the logo BDC – Berlin Document Centre. This is where the personnel dossiers of the members of the NSDAP, the SS and other Nazi organisations were centralised. It is without doubt the largest documentation centre in the world on Nazi war criminals, placed under the authority of the department of state and the American mission in West Berlin. At the time, few people had access to it; you needed rock-solid authorisations to consult and copy the documents that I am flicking through. There was also the internal correspondence of various offices of the CIA in Germany and the headquarters of the agency dealing with the employment of Nazi war criminals.

Towards the end of the war, the American secret services (OSS, G-2, CIC) put in place networks charged with exfiltrating former Nazis whom they wanted to protect or use. War criminals for the most part, they generally figured on the lists, drawn up by the Allies, of Nazi personalities who should be immediately arrested. But in that troubled period, the American secret services decreed that certain of its criminals could be employed in the context of the Cold War, deciding to hide them in the United States so as to keep them away from Soviet influence. In 1949, the American Congress authorised the director of the CIA to bring into the United States immigrants who should never have been admitted because of their past. The CIA Act stipulates, among other provisions, that particular persons could enter the CIA independently of their admissibility in terms of immigration laws or regulations. In the beginning, the CIA's quota was for a hundred people a year; very quickly, however, thousands of other war criminals and former SS men migrated to the United States. The CIA brought them in illegally, inciting them to lie about their past. It is estimated that more than 20,000 former Nazis or their auxiliaries from central Europe took refuge in the United States. In 1978, however, the situation changed dramatically. The American government created the Office of Special Investigations (the OSI), within the Department of Justice, in order to track down the war criminals who had taken refuge in the United States and send them back to their countries, after having stripped them of their American nationality if need be.

But behind the scenes, an organisation of avengers was at work. The one that had welcomed me with open arms. It had already added several rats to its hunting bag.

'We are all children of the Holocaust. Some of us experienced the hell of the camps. That is my case. Others, like you, saw their family decimated. But each of the members of The Owl has an account to settle. That is why I chose them."

This was no longer the jovial Barney speaking. I saw his true face, that of a man gnawed away from the inside by a past that he could never forget.

\*

A few hours later, we were all gathered in Serendipity, a restaurant in eastern Manhattan, not far from Central Park. Classical music, paintings on the walls, sculptures of famous musicians and instruments scattered here and there: in this Mecca of New York life, refinement was the keynote. The room is full to bursting with businessmen and politicians, stockbrokers, wealthy tourists. We were in good company. I had almost forgotten the reason we are in New York. Barney's solemn air as the waiter filled our glasses served to remind me. Before I had even had time to wonder why we were drinking champagne, Barney declared with a mischievous smile:

'There are rats in our yard and it is high time for a clean-out!'

Stunned, I looked all around, convinced that everyone in the room had heard. I met the gaze of Senator Ted Kennedy, who was dining a few tables away. But I quickly calmed down, realising that our neighbours had showed no reaction. No one was giving us any attention. We all lifted our glasses and made a wish for the success of 'Operation Clean-Up'. The evening passed without another allusion to it. Walls have ears, particularly in this kind of place, frequented by the elite of the political class and the American jet-set…

*

The following day, after loading the equipment into Barney's family car, we took to the road. Destination: the tourist site of Hunter Mountain. For the next three hours, we drove through typical American landscapes, vast forests surrounding several villages, streams and rivers. We neared the Catskill Mountains and the little towns became few and far between. The only homes in sight were now miles apart.

The car slowed down and went into a bend to the left, taking a small track between the trees. After a few minutes, here we were in front of a two-storey chalet equipped with every comfort. Rustic but smart, the place was reassuring. At the foot of the chalet, a harmonious mixture of stone and tree trunks, ran a river that transformed into a torrent before losing itself among the fir trees. In the distance could be seen the peaks of the Catskills, which overlook the ski pistes in winter. It was a fine day; New York and its sweltering heat seemed far away. Several cars as well as a caravan were already parked in the yard.

'Everyone is there,' remarked Barney with satisfaction.

The tension grew. It is clear that I was going to have to commit myself, assume a heavy responsibility that I would no longer be able to evade; I was entering a secret organisation with strict rules. We quickly unloaded the car and several minutes later everyone was gathered in the sitting room.

I recognised John, my CIA recruiting sergeant. He was responsible for the technical aspects of the organisation. It is impossible to imagine The Owl without this cheerful 'Yankee' whose exploits in Hanoi caused much havoc in the ranks of the Vietcong. Thanks to him, our organisation got live, and crucial, information, giving it precious advantages over its quarry.

There was Paul, a Green Beret, also a Vietnam veteran; Gerald, a police officer, was a former soldier who was an officer in the Signals Corps; Sean and Harry, two lawyers with precious contacts in the Department of Justice and the bureau for migration; Suzanne, a chemistry expert; Sharon, computer specialist; Roger, an American Marine commando veteran; and finally, of course, Barney and his right-hand woman, his wife Jane, a doctor. The whole group gravitated towards and was organised around this couple.

After several minutes of general excitement, everyone went through into a smaller room, baptized the work room, where we were all given an identical file. Jane served coffee and we began to study the documents in it, following the instructions of John, who gathered and filed them. We had in front of us several photographs of our target, today a respectable retired man with a placid air. We saw him as a younger man, proud and arrogant, posing in the black SS uniform with its skull and crossbones insignia. There were several enlargements of photographs dating from different periods, during the successive stages of the war. Still other documents: photos, maps of several isolated regions of North America, often bordering lakes. Hideouts? This file, carefully prepared over several years, bore witness to our man's suspicious and prudent behaviour. He had chosen to bury himself in the heart of a mountainous region where he could practise his favourite pastimes: fishing, sailing and aviation.

I immersed myself in reading about him.

# THE RECRUIT

SURNAME: Heim

FIRST NAME: Aribert

Born 28 June 1914 in Bad Radkersburg (Austria)

FATHER'S PROFESSION: policeman

MOTHER'S PROFESSION: housewife

Medical studies in Vienna

Enrolled in the SS in spring 1940

Number of SS card: 367 744

HEIGHT: 1.9 metres

DISTINGUISHING MARKS: scar on right cheek

At that time, at the beginning of the 1980s, Aribert Heim was third on the list of the planet's most wanted Nazi war criminals, just behind Josef Mengele, who had gone to ground in Latin America, and Aloïs Brunner, who had been resident in Syria for decades.

Little was known about Heim's role in the Holocaust. A member of the Nazi party who volunteered to join the Waffen SS, after completing his medical studies he was appointed to the camp of Mauthausen, where he arrived on 8 October 1941. He was just 27 years old. In the east, the Einstatzgruppen were engaged in full-scale massacre; by the end of the year, they would have killed almost a million Jews. The concentration and extermination camps were already getting ready to give the Holocaust an industrial edge.

Some 198,000 people were deported to Mauthausen; 118,000 of them were assassinated there. Much has been written about this camp, erected in August 1938 on a hill overlooking the Danube, in the region of Linz, and the largest of the sixty camps in Austria. Much has been written about its gas chambers, about its sadly famous stone quarry surrounded by barbed wire and watchtowers, on the 186 steps of this crater which the inmates, under the barked orders of the SS, had to climb up and down loaded with loose stones, until they died of exhaustion. Much less is known, on the other hand, about the medical experiments carried out under the supervision of, among others, Aribert Heim, whom the survivors describe as 'the most horrific doctor in the camp'. His speciality: 'useless operations'. Karl Lotter, a detainee who was requisitioned to the infirmary, remembered a young Czech brought to the operating theatre with a gangrenous leg. Heim disembowelled him without anaesthetic, messed around with his entrails, sliced off his testicles and dissected one of his kidneys. To practise. One day, according to another witness, Heim put a Viennese Jew in front of a mirror and said to him, 'Look at your nose, the Führer doesn't need that!' The man began to cry and begged for his life. Heim cut his head off, had it boiled, and placed it on his desk, using it as a paperweight. Another time, he carved up one of his victims who bore the tattoo of a boat on his back; his tanned skin served to decorate a lampshade offered to a camp commandant.

Aribert Heim is among those perverted doctors for whom the concentration camps were gigantic laboratories in which they could conduct medical experimentation on human beings without the least hindrance. Everything possible was tried, from vaccination trials to the most insane 'tests' (resistance to cold or to pain). Heim's experiments do not equal in horror those of Dr Mengele in Auschwitz-Birkenau, but they are no less terrifying. He did not hesitate to operate on his guinea pigs without anaesthetic. His 'comparative study' on the mixing of poisons is a monument of its kind. Stopwatch in hand, he tested the speed with which fatal injections into his victims' hearts took effect. A practice that earned him the nickname among Mauthausen's Spanish survivors of 'el banderillero'. In almost two months, 'Dr Death' assassinated several hundred deportees in the name of what he called his 'research'.

Almost nothing is known of Heim's ensuing career in the Waffen SS, which he rejoined after his departure from Mauthausen on 29 November 1941. Captured by the American army on 15 May 1945, he was quickly released, in circumstances that are shrouded in secrecy – there is talk of protection, of services rendered. Nothing explains such indulgence; in fact, the Americans were probably ignorant of who they were dealing with. Arrested at the same time by the British, Josef Mengele was also released without having been identified. The Allies were at that time preoccupied only with the nascent cold war; the capture of Nazi war criminals was not among their immediate concerns.

Whatever the case, Heim thus gained his freedom and settled in Baden-Baden, where he practised medicine for several years without anyone taking issue with him. He opened a health centre aimed at a female clientele. Traced by Nazi hunters, he owed his salvation, yet again, to solid protection. He disappeared on the eve of his arrest in 1962. Since then, he had been under an international arrest warrant. In 1979, Heim was sentenced in absentia to a long prison sentence by a Berlin court.

The man was rich. Very rich. Large transfers of funds from his bank accounts led to a Spanish trail. Certain 'Nazi hunters' such as Simon Wiesenthal believed they had seen him on the Costa Brava where he lived protected by men from the Odessa network. At a certain period, a witness appeared and recounted that he had seen Dr Death strolling peacefully down the streets of a small town. The hunters narrowly missed capturing their prey. He was said to be in Latin America. Or back in Germany. A thick smoke screen covered his tracks.

'He uses a double,' explained Barney. 'Wiesenthal's men, Interpol, the German police, the secret services – everyone is running after a shadow...'

Then, after a silence:

'Aribert Heim lives in the United States. He is less than sixty-five miles away from here, in the Catskills. And we are going to deal with him.'

# CHAPTER 2

# THE LONG CHASE

S EVERAL WEEKS LATER, WHEN THE OPERATION WAS ABOUT TO BEGIN, BARNEY CALLED AN EMERGENCY MEETING: THERE WAS INFORMATION THAT ARIBERT HEIM WAS IN URUGUAY. Witnesses were certain they had seen him. Opinion in the organisation as to what plan to follow was divided; the majority asked for further investigation. Barney talked about disinformation and mentioned the possibility that Heim was again using a double to muddy the waters. The debate got lively and the pitch rose. I intervened:

'I propose we ask the opinion of a third party. Someone beyond challenge: Isser Harel.'

A respectful silence greeted my proposition. Isser Harel was the former chief of the Israeli secret service; it was he who led the capture of Adolf Eichmann in Argentina in 1960.

'But he stopped heading Mossad a long time ago,' says Barney.

'He still has access to vital information about the Nazis. If there is someone on this earth who has information about Aribert Heim, it is him.'

The affair was a delicate one. I preferred not to get hold of him through my contacts inside Mossad, so as to avoid leaks or possible sabotage – the consequences of the inevitable jealousy to which such an operation gives rise. I preferred to go through a very dear friend, Naomi Frankel, a renowned journalist, writer and historian, in whom I had total confidence. Naomi knew Harel personally.

'He is a hard man, not easy. I doubt that he will see you,' she said to me several days later, 'but I'll give it a try.'

Naomi was wrong. Shortly afterwards, she announced with a satisfied smile:

'Harel will see you. Don't talk about me on the phone and above all don't make him angry.'

My friend did not know the details of our operation; she knew that it is to do with the Nazis but nothing more. She asked me no questions and I told her nothing.

*

My first meeting with Harel took place in Tel Aviv, in the Café Oslo, a peaceful place on the southern bank of the Yarkon river. This man, of unassuming appearance and nicknamed 'Little

Isser', was the greatest leader in Mossad's history, to which he owes his worldwide reputation. The meeting was tense. Immediately, I am met with a long monologue. Harel was aggressive, warned me of the risks that would be run in case of failure and of the diplomatic scandal that would result. He shifted around in his seat, agitated. He gave me the impression that he was not at all in favour of what we are doing, a little as if we were planning to uncover one of the best kept secrets of the state of Israel.

'Those rotten Nazis are not worth it,' he said.

Contrary to what he had given me to understand on the phone, Harel was, however, ready to listen to us, even to help us, but on one condition: he wanted to have access to our information. I therefore handed over to him a sample of our files and explained what we had. Harel was visibly impressed; this was the first time he had seen the material I was showing him.

'How did you get these documents?' he asked in an aggressive tone.

I leaned towards the former head of Mossad and murmured:

'We have a CIA official on our team. He has put aside everything he can. A sort of non-refundable debt.'

Harel did not appreciate the joke. He shot a cold look at me and said:

'If that had happened in Israel, I would have hung you from the highest tree in Tel Aviv.'

His manner was so persuasive that I could already feel the rope around my neck.

After that first meeting, I called John in New York.

'Given the kind of chap he is,' I told him, 'it didn't go too badly. He wants to meet you and also to see the rest of our documentation.'

The second meeting took place three days later, in one of the largest luxury hotels in Tel Aviv, to where John had come. The CIA official handed his files to the former head of Mossad.

Without saying a word, Harel flicked through the documents. He paled. When he began talking, he seemed disturbed.

'You've done some good work, you little sods,' he threw out in John's direction. Then, brusquely: 'What do you want from me?'

I cleared my throat.

'We need more information about Aribert Heim. We think that he is in the United States but witnesses affirm they have seen him in Uruguay. What do you think?'

I also took advantage of the occasion to ask him for information about two other war criminals operating in the Balkans, Zobrach and Lichtanker, targets of other operations organised by Barney.

A week later, Harel saw us for the last time. He was a man such as one rarely finds, giving the impression of knowing everything; no one was his equal in transforming words into action. Without ever having been involved in any of the organisation's operational decisions or in any of its activities whatsoever, he nonetheless gave us some information that is decisive for the continuation of the operation.

'Don't waste your time looking for Aribert Heim in Uruguay. Your information is good. He is in the United States.'

Then, after a moment of silence, the small man declared:

'We have never seen each other. These meetings never took place. A piece of advice: don't mess up. If you make the smallest mistake, you will be on your own; everyone will drop you.'

We were at the end of summer 1980.

The chase was about to begin.

*

Barney's files are very complete. Thanks to them we know practically everything about Aribert's Heim's movements in the United States. After his escape from Germany, Dr Death took refuge in Latin America, after a detour in Switzerland then Spain. He arrived in the United States at the end of the 1960s, doubtless by sea. At the moment, he is living on a vast, isolated property situated north of Hunter Mountain, less than sixty-five miles from our chalet. In his service are a handful of men, led by two former members of the Hungarian Nazi group, the Arrow Cross Party. These men are also war criminals who have been wanted since the end of the Second World War. They act as his secretaries, bodyguards and factotums. We know everything about them. We know the type and number of their firearms, as well as the numbers of their gun licences.

In short, we are very well informed about Aribert Heim and his friends. All the data is carefully collected and studied. But getting our hands on our prey is easier said than done. First difficulty: Heim never goes anywhere alone. He is constantly escorted by two armed guerrillas, the most imposing of whom could be taken for his twin brother. Moreover, it is not easy to follow his movements. We do not have an informant in his entourage and it is hardly easy to spy on his whereabouts in the open countryside. Fortunately, thanks to Barney's financial means, we are equipped with the most sophisticated electronic spying equipment: micro-satellite dishes that can capture conversations from dozens of yards away, heat or sound detectors, telephone listening devices... Our arsenal rivals that of the secret services; all that is missing is satellite surveillance. We can follow our target's smallest acts and gestures, even if we cannot always – for logistical reasons – react as quickly as we would like. A long chase is beginning. Taxing. Requiring patience. We need to wait for the right time, the propitious moment to strike.

Once a day, we hold a briefing meeting on the situation, exchanging information and ideas. John is responsible for centralising the electronic intelligence.

'The rat is in the northern part of Hunter Mountain and is going to stay there for a long time,' he says. 'That is where we have to act. We cannot attack his property from the front. It is too well defended and we don't have enough men. We should try to avoid bloodshed – even if we know that is practically impossible... But above all we should capture Heim alive to give him over to his judges. It is they who will decide the hour of his death.'

'So what should we do?'

'We attack when he comes out.'

'There is another possibility. Heim goes gliding. We have followed him to his club, near Westborough. It is a very small club, just a runway with several Cessnas and gliders; there isn't even a control tower. No need to get permission to take off. We could intercept him there.'

John sets out a plan that seems somewhat risky.

'We cannot take him on the airport runway – he goes there with his bodyguards. The only time he is truly alone is in his glider. That is where we will kidnap him.'

Silence in the room. John sees the incredulity on our faces.

'If the weather conditions allow him to get sufficient altitude and to get away from the airport towards wooded regions, we will follow plan number 2, which is to fly close to his plane.'

'And how do we do that? Do we also have a glider?'

'No. It's very simple. We bring a Cessna that we leave in a local aeroclub. We move in when the rat is aboard his glider. We take to the air at the same time as he does; it's easy, you just need a lookout to signal his take-off. Our plane follows his glider and we move in as soon as he stalls, forcing him to make an emergency landing.'

'How?'

'We could sabotage the plane before it takes off. Provoke a breakdown to force him to go down.'

'It's risky. Don't forget we want him alive.'

Hubbub. We are not listening to John any more. His project seems preposterous to us. He begins talking again:

'No, no, a marksman aboard our Cessna puts the rat's glider out of action. He shoots at the empennage, into the wings or at the tail.'

Everyone starts speaking at the same time. John again interrupts us:

'Silence! This plan is the only feasible one. Nothing is easier than hiring a Cessna and in our group we have a least two marksmen.'

Protestations rang out:

'And if the rat is killed during the emergency landing?'

'Once we're on the ground, what do we do? Do we send him a welcoming committee? It will take us hours to get to him.'

John smiles.

'No, that's the whole beauty of the plan. The reception team is on board the Cessna. We localise the rat's glider on the ground, then two of our men make a parachute jump and grab him.'

The project seems insane to me. I don't like it at all. And I am not the only one. There are too many unknowns, too many risks, and too few chances of success. It would need only for the weather conditions to be bad or for there to be other gliders in the area – and God knows there are a lot in that season – for the operation to fail. We need to find something else. Secretly, I pray that the plan will not be implemented. But the reconnaissance begins. John brings a Cessna, kept on a little runway not far from Westborough. Three of us are designated: a marksman and two parachutists. I confess that I am quite happy not to be part of the commando. The attack begins.

One Wednesday evening: action stations. The telephone monitoring tells us that Aribert Heim intends to go flying the following day. The first phase of the plan is immediately launched. The surveillance of the Westborough runway is reinforced. As I get up that morning, I look at the sky. The weather is not good: it is cloudy, with the possibility of rain.

The radio crackles:

'Owl one, this is Owl four. The rat has left his nest. I repeat: the rat has left his nest.'

Phase two: the three men of the commando take their place aboard the Cessna. They have time. Our target will not be in his Cessna for another half-hour.

Ten minutes later, another radio message:

'He is not alone.'

Aribert Heim has taken his seat in the glider with his bodyguard. It is an eventuality we have envisaged; until then, our target has flown alone, but his glider being a two-seater, we have had to take that possibility into account. We would therefore have to get rid of the bodyguard – in the air or on the ground. Heim's glider is attached to the plane in front, ready to be towed. As the coupling lifts into the air, our Cessna is already in the sky within firing range of the Westborough runway. Our men see the rat take off. They see the glider buffeted about by the wind and wait for it to be detached before moving in.

Suddenly, however, the plane and its glider do an about-turn: because of the weather conditions, our target has cancelled his flight. Several hours later, back in the chalet, John bows to our arguments. His plan is too risky and involves too many uncertainties. He agrees to abandon it.

Barney had planned to stay at the chalet just a few days; given the circumstances, he decides to prolong his stay so as to play a part in the implementation of the operation. The reconnaissance around Heim's home is strengthened. From now on, surveillance will be constant; there will always be someone on the lookout.

We again envisage a frontal attack. Not knowing what detection and defense system the Nazi has at his disposal, we abandon the idea of penetrating his house and draw up plans for intercepting him in the forest during one of his rare outings. We plan ambushes in several places where he regularly walks.

Our group is divided into three teams and two special squads, nicknamed 'the veterinarians', equipped with weapons with silencers, chloroformed darts, very powerful binoculars, communication equipment, camouflage materials and camping bags containing food and various tools. It is decided that once we have taken the rat, we should split up, taking the necessary precautions so as not to be seen. Each one of us should go, alone, to a meeting place agreed in advance, within seven days. We also decide on special codes to be used in case of emergency.

Then begin long days of waiting, lulled by boredom and

punctuated by tours of reconnaissance and inspection of places of possible ambush. To distract ourselves from the waiting and the nervousness, we train regularly: running through the woods and physical exercises occupy our bodies and minds. From time to time, we assemble for shooting sessions in recesses of the wood, using special silencers. These sessions always end with a careful cleaning of the spot: we pick up the ejected cartridges, wipe over our traces and disappear into the forest.

One morning, I get up in an excellent mood. The tension seems to have left my body. I stay several moments in front of the chalet, facing the forest, giving myself over to an irresistible sensation of well-being. There is an ideal temperature and a soft light; the day contains promise. After a hearty breakfast, we leave in groups of two. We go deep into the woods for yet another reconnaissance, preceded by our scouts. Suddenly, our radio crackles. It is John:

'Owl two, the rat is advancing in your direction.'

My heart leaps. Suddenly the atmosphere is electric. The transmitted message is clear. The moment has arrived.

Nerves on edge, I catch hold of my binoculars and scrutinise the undergrowth. Everything seems calm. Shrubs, bushes, tree trunks, a deer moving, more trees, and path, and then... I freeze. There! I see him! But he is not alone. One of his henchmen is accompanying him. There also seems to be a family with him: a woman, a man, three children. I focus on the man who is in the middle of the group. Very tall, dressed like a hockey player, dark and handsome. Moving with self-assurance, he reminds me of a movie star. At first, I see only his left profile but when he turns towards his neighbour to tell him something, I see the scar on the right side of the lip.

It is him.

It is Aribert Heim.

A burst of adrenalin: it is my first visual contact with the target. At his side, a man who seems more a member of his family than a bodyguard. There are only two of us. We are armed and determined, the element of surprise is on our side; it is perhaps workable.

'What do you think?' I say to Paul in a single breath.

'Don't know.'

'Do we try?'

'We'll have to see... We'll let him come and we'll take it from there. I'll warn the others. If there is an opening, we'll move. Otherwise, we'll wait for reinforcements.'

'To all Owls, this is Owl two. The rat is in sight. He is not alone. I repeat, he is not alone. With him is another rat and five civilians,' Paul breathes into his walkie-talkie before giving our position.

Aribert Heim and his companions peacefully continue their promenade in the forest. I imagine that their topic of conversation is the impressive nature that surrounds them and its resemblance to paradise. They do not know how close hell is for them... An inner prayer: thank you, God, for having sent us our prey. I glance over to Paul, the Green Beret, my companion-in-arms. He too is stressed. Concentrated. A predator on the alert. It will be his task to deal with Heim. I for my part will have to cover him in case of problems. And there will be problems – starting with the presence of three charming youngsters.

'We don't touch the children,' Paul murmurs to me.

We had already discussed among ourselves what to do in case of Aribert Heim being accompanied by the women, children or men of his family. It was more than a possibility, Dr Death rarely venturing out without his loved ones. We had therefore taken the decision to intervene as soon as that was possible, independent of the number or type of people accompanying him. Armed intervention against a target who was himself ferociously guarded would inevitably pose a risk to everyone present at the place of ambush, women and children included.

I study the group advancing towards us through my binoculars. The joyful cries of the children skipping along the path do not affect my resolution. I weigh them up against the screams of pain of the little martyrs of the Holocaust, wondering what the reaction of these joyous children would be if they were told what their grandfather's 'medical' speciality was in Mauthausen... What would they think of Grandpa Ari if they knew he had had no equal when it came to injecting diesel into the hearts of his victims, with a sure and resolute hand? What would they say about this handsome old man who had worked zealously for the destruction of the Jewish people, massacring men, women and children without a shadow of hesitation or remorse? How would they react if they read the terrible judgement of a German tribunal which, several months earlier, in 1979, had sentenced him for war crimes after hearing the survivors of his experiments? Dr Death, however, scorns these judgements. So be it — if human justice cannot punish him, we will do so ourselves.

The voices are getting closer. The crystal-clear laughter of the children rings out, louder and louder. It is the moment of truth. I tense my muscles. But suddenly the footsteps cease, the group stops and we hear the sound of hooves hammering against the ground. A group of riders is galloping through the wood in our direction. This was all we needed.

Next to me, I hear Paul swearing. We are far enough away from the horses for them not to sense us. Above all, we mustn't move or do anything that could give away our presence. Hidden by the trees, we see three riders coming at a gallop; black riding hats and jackets over white shirts and ties, pale jodhpurs in black boots, they seem right out of a riding manual. The horse in front, a superb black thoroughbred mare, streaked with white bands of sweat, has seen Aribert Heim and his family. His rider too. The horses slow down, move to a trot and then to a walk, before stopping level with the walkers.

I am furious. I feel like screaming out.

The lead horseman exchanges a few words with the oldest of the women, doubtless the mother of the children. They all obviously know each other. Suddenly, he gets down from his mount and shakes everyone's hand, including those of the admiring children surrounding him. He says a few words to one of the boys, then lifts him from the ground and sticks him in the saddle. Everyone applauds the little adventurer. Soon, the other horsemen get down from their horses in their turn, so as to put the other two children in the saddle. The youngsters are impressed. Mad with rage and helplessness, I look through the binoculars one last time to scrutinise the face of the old man who has once again escaped us. A good rifle with a telescopic sight would enable me to get him without problem from where I am. But the Owl has other plans for him.

The three horsemen advance, each holding their mount by the reins, the children still in the saddle. Aribert Heim and his family follow, talking cheerfully. Our target moves off into the distance, unaware of the danger that had been awaiting him.

'Owl one, this is Owl two. The rat is returning to his den,' murmurs Paul into his walkie-talkie. 'Shit!'

Disillusioned, Paul and I are silent for what feels like an age. The tension that has been accumulating for more than an hour falls. I finally sigh:

'That's life. There will be other disappointments like that before we achieve our goal.'

'Thanks for your encouragement. Are you on our side or his?' Paul retorts, giving me a violent poke in the back that almost pushes me out of our hiding place.

Once we are sure we are alone, we emerge from our shelter

after having put our weapons and binoculars away in our backpacks. We still need to walk for two good hours to get back to the vehicle that will take us back to the chalet, at the other end of the forest.

*

Several hours later, we are all reassembled in our retreat. We hold a business meeting, a debriefing of the morning's events and a reassessment of the situation. We are overwhelmed with questions. We were expecting the rat and his bodyguard, instead of which we fell upon a family outing.

'The new arrivals left last night,' explains John. 'We missed them. I was able to make a few phone calls. My contacts have been hard at it. Let's first take care of the henchman who accompanies the rat during his walk. Danny has described him to us.'

John gets out a photo; it is him.

'One of the rat's favourite bodyguards. A bloodthirsty type. Always armed.'

John consults his notes:

'Ah, here we are… No gun licence… an 11 mm Colt and a 9mm Smith & Wesson… enormous pieces… An element to take into consideration in the context of a new plan. Fortunately you didn't take any action. It could have turned into a bloodbath.'

'Okay, next this one,' went on John, getting out the photo of the other man whom I had seen beside Aribert Heim. 'The family man. He is the grandson of the rat's closest friend. A friendship forged in the ranks of the SS. For all these years they have kept a close relationship and spent a lot of time together, until the disappearance of the friend in question, in Latin America. In fact, the grandson and his family constitute the rat's whole universe, since the mysterious disappearance of his own family in Europe, at the end of the Second World War. The grandson belongs to a secret neo-Nazi group and he may serve as contact between his father – doubtless hiding in Venezuela – and the rat. We are collecting documents on the subject. Something to be followed up.'

Finally, John gets out a photo of the children's mother.

'She is responsible for the failure of the operation: she is a riding instructor, well known in New York state. One of the riders, the one that was in front, is a member of the same riding club. He recognised her, which explains the "touching" meeting that ruined all our plans.'

Barney then sets out the news from the team responsible for listening surveillance, which is not good.

'Our men have intercepted bits of a conversation that Heim had late last night with his bodyguard. The rat intends to go to Quebec for the winter. He will stay in Canada for several months, with friends originally from Germany.'

We look at each other in consternation. Why is Aribert Heim on his guard? What is he suspicious of? Has he spotted us? Have we made a mistake liable to expose the operation? There is another, even more worrying, hypothesis: that Aribert Heim has friends in very high places in the American administration. He has perhaps been tipped off.

'We must proceed with maximum caution,' says Barney. 'You have done excellent work until now. We must carry on and not be discouraged.'

John goes further:

'We must be patient and carry out every step meticulously – that's the only way to reach our target.'

I smile. It is like a game of chess, in which the human pieces are advancing cautiously on the chessboard, where the one who gains an advantage and manages to keep it ends up the winner, while the one who makes a mistake is punished with a resounding checkmate. Now, the game has been going on for months. We have the advantage of surprise, but we have not managed to take any pawns... Each time we think we've got the king, he evades us. Since the incident of the horse riders, Aribert Heim has not emerged from his hiding place. There is only one thing left for us to do: wait. Wait until the next turnaround in the situation. In practice, that means tedious hours of ambush, watching, tension, new plans and frustration. We spend long days waiting, nerves on edge, for something to happen, struggling against fatigue and unfavourable weather conditions.

The days go by. Our quarry is stationary. On the rare occasions he moves, we miss him. In September, the forest is decked out in its autumn colours; the mosaic of dead leaves gives it an enchantingly rural feel and our ambushes become much more pleasant. Alas, the season does not last long; soon cold and snow begin to attack the region and our commando changes its wardrobe – we resemble white owls, in our fleece suits. Everything is white; we continue our ambush as ghosts.

*

Weeks had passed. We were now in the beginning of winter. One Friday evening, we were sitting around the Sabbath dinner table in our chalet-retreat-headquarters. Barney had just said the blessing, expressing gratitude for being able to satisfy his hunger and handing out a morsel of bread to each of us. Over the first course, he declared solemnly:

'We have been invited to a wedding in Detroit next week. It is an important event and we cannot disappoint the happy couple.'

I could not imagine anything better; I was delighted that I will be able to have a change of scene, far from the forest of Hunter Mountain. Aribert Heim could wait. In any case, he seemed to have made up his mind to hibernate. From our telephone tapping, we had learnt that he had postponed his trip to Quebec. We needed only to leave a small team here to ensure that our target remains available.

'It's a Jewish wedding? In that case,' I said to Barney, 'there is always a little orchestra. If you can get hold of a trumpet for me, I'll play you "My Yiddishe Mama", that's a promise!'

'It's a deal!'

In the middle of the week, we left for Detroit in a hired single-engine plane. As we got further and further away from Hunter Mountain, our mood became increasingly cheerful and teasing. As if an invisible dam had exploded, freeing in one go an immense energy, we were overtaken by long bouts of hilarious laughter, without really knowing what they were about. It was impossible to calm down. It was a kind of rebirth, as if we had rediscovered the real world after spending long months in a nightmare. Today, I remain convinced that only the intervention of the Creator allowed us to land on the Detroit runway, none of us being operational at the moment of landing. The plane hit the ground violently and came to a stop after three very impressive kangaroo jumps. By saving us that day, luck abandoned Aribert Heim.

The control tower wanted an explanation for the bizarre landing that they had just witnessed. Not without humour, the air traffic controller commented that the Cessna had doubtless filled up on fuel 'at Johnny Walker's'... The remark did not help us calm down. The airport manager summoned us to reprimand us for our behaviour – but he too was quickly contaminated by our hilarity. Several hours later, just before the wedding ceremony, our little group had finally become serious again.

We turned up at one of the biggest hotels in the town. Guests were streaming from the lobby towards the rooms in which the reception was taking place. We made our way through the crowd in evening dress. Our hunting territory in the Catskills seemed very far away. At the end of the room, an orchestra was playing the standard Hassidic tunes.

As soon as I went in, I saw her. Jo. A young Canadian, the cousin of one of my friends, an Israeli studying in New York. She belonged to a family of Holocaust survivors, originally from Germany. I had first met her in New York several months earlier – when I had already been sensible to her charms... We took each other's hands like old friends, then I hugged her and she deposited a kiss on my cheek. We gazed at each other. Her beautiful black eyes were slightly moist, showing that she was as perturbed as I was. Both stunned by the violence of this meeting, we suddenly felt in need of fresh air and left the room. In the lift, we fell into each other's arms, our lips and bodies seeking each other and my feverish hands discovering her fine outline. I don't know how long we stayed there... All I knew is that it seemed like a delightful eternity.

Several words murmured in the ear, a last furtive kiss and then we joined the other guests in the room. We did not leave each other all evening – and I felt certain that we would never leave each other. I knew that from then on she would be with me in the most difficult moments or during the most delicate missions; she would fill me with energy during the long hours of ambush, when mind and senses fight against cold and fatigue. I was certain that, when my mission was accomplished, she would become my wife. I was already imagining my life with her and dreaming of our children.

But I also knew that I would never be able to talk to her about Aribert Heim. That I would be forced to hide the most important part of my life from her. Impossible to reveal the existence of The Owl to her, to tell her about our discussions, our avengers' enthusiasm, about this feeling of accomplishing a *mitsva*, a good action for our community and, beyond that, for humanity. She would never know about the waiting, the mounting adrenalin, the chase. And when it was all over, when Heim was no more, she would never know that, behind the scenes, a handful of Jews had again avenged the victims of the Holocaust. The world of intelligence is a world apart, one that requires delicate handling and is full of danger. I could not run the risk of accidentally letting information slip. At that time, I thought that the existence of The Owl would have to be secret for ever, to protect the security of its members who, over 20 years, had eliminated dozens of Nazi war criminals, and to protect the security of missions to come. At that time, the beginning of the 1980s, tens of thousands of those responsible for the massacre of the Jews were still alive. After the mysterious disappearances of former Nazis, certain people must have realised that an organisation of exterminators was operating from the shadows; confirming that suspicion was an impossible step to take. The law of silence was the best protection for The Owl, the fearsome predator of an endangered species. I knew that this could get in the way of a possible future together, but my first loyalty was to my mission.

'We were beginning to worry!'

Barney's face lit up with a mischievous smile; he had interrupted my daydreaming and my amorous tête-à-tête.

'She is gorgeous, your girlfriend...' he saw fit to add, making Jo blush as I introduced her to my friends – who hastened to lift their glasses to her.

'And your promise?' went on Barney, showing me the trumpeter on the stage.

'I haven't forgotten, don't worry...'

And so it was that I suddenly found myself on stage under a barrage of applause. I was given a trumpet. The orchestra began playing 'My Yiddishe Mama' and a profound silence fell over the room. This piece begins with a trumpet solo, electrifying the audience; the next bit is even more moving and some of the guests, particularly the oldest ones, were on the verge of tears. This poignant air always made me think of the Jewish communities of central Europe, the *shtels* – of their life before the war, and their destruction. For some time, however, whenever I played or heard it, another image was superimposed on that of the destroyed ghettoes: that of Aribert Heim, who was one of those responsible for their destruction – Heim as I had seen him through my binoculars, during a family walk one fine summer's morning in the Catskills.

The reception went on late into the night, when the guests finally left. We returned to our rooms, tired but with almost no time to sleep; at dawn, we would have to leave for the airport to go back to Hunter Mountain, where much work awaited us. We did not forget that for an instant, even at a celebratory party and even at a wedding. In the lift, Barney hugged me and said:

'Thank you, thank you… You kept your promise and you moved us to tears. I will never forget it.'

I was lost for words. The lift came to a stop; I said to Barney that I was going to say my farewells to Jo.

'Don't hurry,' he replied with a big smile, before the door closed again.

*

In the early morning, I am back at the airport with my friends who are busying themselves with the last details of the flight. Barney fills in the necessary papers and puts the logbook up to date. Meanwhile, I carry out the first checks of the outside of the aeroplane. The little group gets in the Cessna and Barney starts up the engine. I take my place next to him, on the right.

'Permission to take off,' Barney requests the control tower.

'Permission granted. Good luck!'

This return flight is different from the one here. This time, the atmosphere is serious, reserved and the tension only mounts as we get closer to Hunter Mountain. The few words we exchange are about the mission; no one mentions the reception of the previous day, as if it had all been nothing but a dream. I am the only one who is still allowing himself to dwell on his feelings and happiness – I think of Jo…

The forest that we can now see through the window gradually

brings me back to a still distant reality: these woods suddenly seem welcoming, even romantic, and again I feel impatient to fufil the mission that I have taken on.

'Is everything okay?'

Barney's low voice makes me lose the thread of my thoughts. He winks at me:

'I don't like your silence at all...'

I smile.

'You have an hour left to get back in touch with reality,' says Roger. 'After that, we won't have a minute to ourselves.'

We all know he is right.

The little New York State airport is now only five minutes' flight away. The plane slowly descends in neutral and the wheels drop down onto the densely compacted grass of the runway. I tear myself once and for all from my daydreams and also come in to land, ready to confront Dr Death and his men.

Suzanne is there to greet us in the landing zone with a smile. A woman of principle, she is very cultivated, an idealist with a remarkably open mind. A great professional of intelligence, she is one of the pillars of the team. The pleasure of our greetings over, we once again take to the road, this time in the Chevrolet, in the direction of the forest and our headquarters. Suzanne brings us up to date on Heim's activities:

'Nothing new under the sun. He is still not going out. His men do the shopping. In terms of the telephone, nothing interesting. Private calls. The rat is hibernating and nothing indicates that he is ready to leave.'

'That doesn't surprise me,' said Barney.

But the fact that Aribert Heim isn't moving doesn't mean that we can do the same. There is no question of waiting, arms folded, for Dr Death finally to make up his mind to leave his den. No sooner have we arrived back at the chalet than Barney reorganises the groups. This time, I am teamed up with John.

Late that evening, when we are in the middle of work, Suzanne says to me with her marvellous smile and in a kindly tone:

'It seems that everything is for the best in the best of all possible worlds for you...'

'How do you mean?'

'Leave him alone,' intervenes Paul in a mocking voice. 'Can't you see he's in love?'

Suzanne leans against my shoulder seductively:

'When you have the time, teach me how it's done.'

'How what is done?'

'How to fall in love, you idiot!'

And with that she blows me a kiss.

Everyone bursts out laughing and Jane adds:

'You must go to Detroit more often. You bring a good vibe back with you!'

That night, I find it hard to get to sleep and I hope that Heim, who is less than sixty-five miles away from us, is also spending his night tossing and turning in his bed.

Eight o'clock in the morning. The routine begins again. Sitting around the table on the ground floor for breakfast, we study the programme for the three days to come. Two hours later, we are in the thick of it. Suzanne, Paul, Roger and I are taking part in an exhausting training session; to begin, a six-mile run along a steep mountain path. During these sessions, we never use the same itinerary two days running, as much out of concern for discretion as to break the daily monotony. Back in the chalet, we finish off our exercise with the obstacle course created by Paul and Gerald in one of the clearings on the property. Still at racing pace, we climb up the 'soldier's wall', scale rocks and descend by sliding along the length of a cable to end with a jump of several yards into the river. After which, we initiate ourselves – an apprenticeship as exhausting as it is impressive – in the art of kayak canoeing. Roger, an ex-American Marine, had attached four kayaks to the bed of the fast mountain stream that runs near the house with strong elastic belts that we stretch to the maximum while twisting around like maniacs. At least these instruments of torture contribute to a marked improvement in our physical condition and endurance.

The training sessions, which also include instruction in hand-to-hand fighting, go on for four punishing hours. We perfect our shooting techniques by trying out the most diverse positions – lying on the side of our faces, or while running, in defence or attack mode, on foot or moped, in a car or on a speedboat. We also train from hired small aircraft, helicopters or microlights. Once in the air, we open fire in turn on to targets that we have put in place the day before, hidden throughout the forest; we empty our chargers on to canoes or little boats tied to the banks of one of the large isolated lakes of the region. We also undertake underwater diving manoeuvres.

Handling the kayaks forms the most intense part of our training because we have discovered that Aribert Heim and his men criss-cross the lakes in interminable fishing sessions. Silent and easy to hide, the kayak is also very common in that region; its use rouses no suspicion. We ply our oars for hours across the lakes and rivers, sometimes feeling as though we are part of the American Marine commando.

All our leading-edge equipment, our means of transport (planes, helicopters), our electronic espionage systems and our state-of-the-art weapons – all of that would be nothing without our fierce determination. These training sessions are punctuated by moments of exhilaration. Rarely has a group been so closely bonded by physical activity and the desire to accomplish its mission. Our performances are astonishing. My friends are made of the stuff of heroes and to work with them is pure pleasure. And then, when we have to dig to the very bottom of our reserves, during every additional stride, every press-up, every minute spent in the water or the cold, we know that our efforts are taking us a little closer to the moment of truth: the capture of Dr Aribert Heim.

In the afternoon, we study the precious documents and the hundreds of photographs that John has procured – I don't know how. There are images taken by the SS before and during the Second World War and other more recent ones, taken in the United States. Barney and John are the only ones who know the source of this intelligence. We guess that they come from the secret archives of the CIA and the FBI. In truth, the team is not really concerned with the origin of information. We have complete trust in John. Our group includes three former American intelligence officers, Gerald, Sean and Harry; their contacts with the ranks of the administration, who are delighted to contribute to our hunt of Nazi refugees in America, provide us, for free, with the complementary documentation we need.

One afternoon we come across a series of photos immortalising the meeting, in an upstate New York forest, between Aribert Heim and two elderly men. One of whom seems familiar to us. We are sure we have already seen him. But where? John throws another file onto the table.

'It looks like William Patrick, "Willi". He emigrated from Germany shortly before the Second World War. During the war, he served in the Navy. Since then he has lived on Long Island, a model citizen, it seems. He's Hitler's nephew, the son of his half-brother Alois.'

'But I thought that William Patrick had publicly repudiated his uncle? He fought against him, didn't he?'

'He did.'

'What are William Patrick and Aribert Heim doing together?'

'Don't waste your time, it's a dead end,' cuts in John. 'The CIA has already looked into it.'

We reviewed the other photographs. In them we see Aribert Heim and his acolytes, again wearing the black uniform of the SS. Sometimes we find ourselves staring at certain photos in silence, almost as if we were drawing on these men's disdainful air and their immortalised arrogance in these images, taken at the height of their career as war criminals, to renew our avenging zeal. These documents, meticulously assembled over decades, are enough to establish their guilt and that of the other executioners. Around the table, our little group scrutinises the images for hours on end. Finally we bring our research to an end, carrying out what we call in our jargon an 'enriching', a synthesis of all the reference material. We now have to hand all the data necessary for the implementation of an operational plan.

# CHAPTER 3
# THE SEVEN LAKES

I N THE DISTANCE, AN OWL HOOTS IN THE CATSKILLS NIGHT. WE LOOK AT EACH OTHER. Smiles. A good omen. Driving with all the lights off, the four-wheel drive has brought us deep into the middle of the forest, several dozen miles from Aribert Heim's property. We collect our backpacks and activate our nocturnal vision equipment, then make off into the wood, in a south, south-east direction, towards the rat's den. John and I are about to disappear into the heart of the forest for several long days, on permanent lookout, taking notes while waiting for Heim finally to make an appearance. This time, it is much colder and from time to time several flakes of snow float above our heads.

We have just finished our turn on guard duty within shooting distance of Aribert Heim's home. We train our binoculars on the iron gate of the property and then the garage, the deserted courtyard, the entrance and finally the outside. To distract ourselves from the boredom, we immerse ourselves in observing the flora and fauna of Hunter Mountain forest. We naturalists would be virtually capable of writing some of those long articles that are the delight of erudite readers of scientific magazines. Forced to remain absolutely immobile, we are equipped with nothing but our binoculars when we spot those hordes of animals; we can soon predict their movements, defending their territory with admirable determination... I still think with particular tenderness of the squirrels, prepared to do anything to protect their young from a predator. Their surprising energy and ingenuity when they jump with great speed from the ground to the trees, then from branch to branch, is in striking contrast to our passivity. Jealous of these little rodents, we are reduced to dreaming of trading places with them, if only for a few minutes to allow us to bring the circulation back into our legs.

The hours go by. Nothing to report – other than the brief appearance of an enormous tarantula, terrifying John and me... We begin to tell ourselves that we would do better to change tactics. Until now, our movements have depended on Aribert Heim's routine and movements. This waiting could go on for a long time and risk ruining all our plans. We need to take an initiative, any initiative, to force him out of his hole. In the present circumstances, it is impossible to get our hands on him. The instructions given by the organisation – to leave no traces and not to put innocent people in danger – make our task vastly more difficult. On the other hand, if the Butcher of Mauthausen moves as a result of a provocation from us, it will doubtless be difficult for us to react in the short term. Nevertheless, we do not immediately reject the idea of flushing out our prey. We have the means not to lose trace of him and to trap him in any place whatever on earth.

Since the horse riders incident, however, Aribert Heim does not venture out of his property, which is protected by several electronic systems. Every movement in the immediate surroundings is recorded and reported. If a stranger approaches the iron gates, an armed man immediately appears to greet him. Throughout our period of surveillance of the house, we never see Heim near the gates or the mailbox. It is as though Dr Death has sensed our presence.

Shortly before nightfall, a car appears at the entrance – as expected. The gate opens, the vehicle drives to the front steps and stops and a little man holding a briefcase gets out. The man enters our prey's lair, emerging shortly afterwards and leaving again in his car. I radio base to communicate the licence number. Half an hour later, we hear Suzanne's soft voice telling us in our earpierces:

'It was a doctor's car. Someone at the rat's is ill.'

'If it's him, I hope he's not going to snuff it before the time we've appointed for him,' murmurs John before cutting off the communication.

Night falls over the Catskills. In several hours, we will be relieved. It is a full moon; the starry sky is incredibly clear. Before going to sleep in our turn, we contemplate the stars and map out, in hushed tones, new plans of action.

Eight o'clock in the morning. An elbow poke; John wakes me up with a start.

'Things are happening.'

A car is coming out of the garage. In the courtyard, there is a flurry of activity. Ten minutes later, the gates open for a car that takes the road into the town. John follows it with his binoculars. He has identified the chauffeur:

'It's Harold.'

One of Aribert Heim's trusted men. They were together in Mauthausen. I communicate to headquarters the description of the vehicle and its direction. Our equipment is scrambled thanks to an algorithm developed by NSA, the most secret of the American secret services. Although we are certain of the inviolability of our radio communications, we talk in coded language. Two precautions are better than one.

One of our men, Gerald, tails the car without difficulty until it parks in a town situated several dozen miles away in front of a drugstore. He parks in his turn and, with a nonchalant air, goes into the pharmacy. Harold, a huge, imposing individual, is facing the counter. He is mechanically fingering his wallet as he waits for the pharmacist to finish preparing the prescription. Gerald observes the scene while pretending to look for a medicine on one of the shelves; seizing a packet, he goes over to the till to make his purchase and waits in the queue behind Harold. He glances at what medicine the latter is buying and makes out, among other products, powerful antibiotics and analgesics. Gerald suddenly understands why Aribert Heim no longer goes out; it is he who is ill.

Crisis meeting at our headquarters. Gerald lists the drugs he saw on the counter. Those of us who have a little medical knowledge understand.

'The rat is very ill. He has a serious infection and is in a lot of pain.'

'Let him suffer. But not kick the bucket. Not before we decide.'

John and I return to our guard duty until the end of the week, hoping that Aribert Heim will have a speedy recovery. Nothing would have given us more pleasure than to see him walking in the forest again. But our hopes are disappointed and the week goes by with us waiting in vain. Same thing for the team that relieves us.

\*

To give me a change of scenery and break the routine of the guard duty shifts and training sessions, I regularly spend the weekend in New York, in a little apartment in Forest Hills, an area of Queens, not far from where my best friend lives: Giora, whom I met during a pilot training course in the Israeli air force.

# THE SECRET EXECUTIONERS

Republic airport in Long Island has long been our second home. We used to meet each other there whenever we had any free time; it was our starting base for an aerial discovery of the east coast. There was not a single landing run, in concrete or grass, that we had not honoured. Our speciality: hedgehopping flights underneath bridges. More rarely, as a challenge, we would undertake downward nose dives before suddenly straightening the plane just before it hit the ground or else fly in formation and at very high speeds between the walls of natural gorges. I have no secrets from Giora, my friend and brother. A genuine, devoted man of the kind one rarely meets, he would be a choice recruit for The Owl. With Barney's permission, I tell him about the organisation's activities. As I expect, an enthusiastic Giora proves keen to join us. Patience. His time has not yet come. The Owl will have the opportunity to use my friend's piloting talents, on both the east and the west coasts of the United States.

Whenever I am in New York, I let off steam in one fell swoop after the accumulated fatigue of long days of lookout. New York is my cultural and social outlet; I rejoin civilisation and fill up on cinema, theatre and concerts, with a predilection for Carnegie Hall, where I manage to forget about Aribert Heim for a few moments. This wretched Nazi is hardly ever out of my thoughts; I am possessed, I constantly see his image in my mind's eye. I eat, sleep and breathe Aribert Heim. I know that I will not have any rest until the Butcher of Mauthausen is captured... I am not the only one with this condition; the

other members of the organisation are affected by the same
obsessional symptoms.

*

'Hi, Danny! *Shabbat shalom!* Good to see you. How was your
weekend in New York? I hope you used it to get some rest
because there is going to be work to do.'

It is a cheerful Barney who greets me on the front steps that
Saturday evening.

'I called you because there is some news; come on,' he says
to me, leading me into the ground floor sitting room library. I
am surprised to see four other members of The Owl: Sean,
Harry, Suzanne and Sharon.

'Change of programme,' announces Barney. 'Aribert Heim's
health has clearly improved. He was laid up in bed with a
serious intestinal infection but the medicine brought by Harold
has done wonders. A few hours ago, Dr Death telephoned
some friends, the Rudys, who live very near the Seven Lakes
nature reserve in New Jersey. He is going to visit them and is
already talking about taking up fishing and sailing, his favourite
sports, again. Paul and John arrive in town tomorrow. Apart
from Roger and Gerald, who will stay here to cover things, we
will all meet back here tomorrow, Sunday. Who knows?
Perhaps we will be successful this time? I have a good feeling
about it.'

The following morning, we gather again at Barney's.

Relaxed, happy, delighted that the chase was starting up again. The mood of rejoicing jostles for position with a certainty that our luck is finally starting to change. Barney explains to us that we need to change plan. In the Catskills, the topography plays against us. We can intercept Aribert Heim only during one of his walks in the forest – a risky operation, as we have seen. In the Seven Lakes, it would be both easier and more difficult. We plan to seize the Butcher of Mauthausen while he is sailing or fishing. He will certainly be accompanied and we will have to neutralise his escorts. But at least we do not run the risk of being interrupted by inopportune riders or walkers.

A delicate problem remains. Our plan cannot be carried out everywhere. Everything will depend on exactly where Aribert Heim is going to go. Each of the seven lakes of the nature reserve is a different size: the smallest ones do not lend themselves to ambushes, their banks being too close together to operate away from prying eyes. On the other hand, the largest lake is well designed for a rapid, efficient action, because of its size and the thickness of the forest bordering it. We can only wait, hoping that Aribert Heim will venture onto the big lake during his stay. Everything will depend on this eventuality.

Barney owns two outboard motorboats, which he puts at our disposition. We pick up the first on Long Island. The second is anchored in Shipshead Bay, the marina in Brooklyn. On board, we find the equipment we need, including diving suits – invaluable protection against icy lake waters – cans of spare fuel, pieces of lead for weighting down, a towing cable which promises to be our most valuable piece of equipment; in addition, there is the electronic apparatus with which John is going to equip our two racers. For his part, thanks to his contacts, Roger has procured two US Navy surplus 'seals' – little motorised engines designed to propel underwater divers through the water at great speed. Three days later, we are ready. We hitch up the outboard motorboats to our four-wheel drive and wait for the green light to come from the lookout team who have remained as the rearguard in the Catskills. But Heim has delayed his departure. He cannot yet have fully recovered from his infection.

There is a sense of potential action in the air. But a little voice deep inside me, which I cannot succeed in stifling, tells me that things are not going to happen as planned, that we are gearing up for serious difficulties. A premonition? A fear? Pessimism? It was in any case impossible to tell my comrades of my doubts. So I turn to my 'Canadian compass', Jo, in the vain hope of distracting myself from my fears. At the other end of the line, her voice has an energising and pacifying effect on me. Jo knows nothing of my activities but from the beginning of the conversation, she has the feeling that I am hiding something from her.

'Danny, what has happened to you? You're different from usual. You don't seem yourself. What's going on?'

I need to speak to her. She must know. So that she can share my anxieties. But how to tell her that a manhunt now occupies the majority of my time? How to explain that getting close to the target fills me with as much terror as anticipation? I cannot confide in the woman I love and I am forced to lie to her.

'Nothing, just a touch of the blues. That's why I'm ringing you.'

'Are you sure everything's okay?'

'Yes, don't worry. I just felt an enormous desire to hear your voice...'

*

Two weeks later, John informs us that Aribert Heim is finally preparing to leave for the Seven Lakes. The gleam of the hunter begins to shine in Barney's eyes. We split up into four small mobile teams. Roger, Paul, Sean and I form team number one, responsible for intercepting Heim. We settle ourselves near one of the banks of the large lake, in a spot suitable for secret activities, far from curious eyes. Barney and Jane are at the command post in team number two, backed up by John who is working independently throughout the whole of the lakes region. Gerald and Sharon, team number three and responsible for reconnaissance, patrol virtually everywhere around the three small lakes; team four, Harry and Suzanne, are watching out for the other three. The four teams put up their tents. The camp looks in every way like that of holidaymakers. From now on, contact between the teams will take place only by crypted radio.

During this time, surveillance of Aribert Heim's residence has begun. The routine of telephone listening and tailings has begun again. John is tracking our target, following each of his movements inside and outside his home. On the Wednesday after our arrival, he intercepts a conversation between Heim and his hosts in which there is talk of a boat, a small sailing boat that the Rudys regularly put at the disposal of their distinguished guest.

'The sailboat is anchored in my region of New York. It will be here for several days and you are welcome to use it,' declared Aribert Heim's friend. 'Our other friends are also due to come, as arranged. You can all go out onto the lake to relax'

This was the information that we needed. Heim intends to go out onto the big lake. Our preparations were well founded and the hunting ground is ideal. From now on, John follows the sailboat's slightest movements, charted on a map until its arrival in the region. Just in case, we continue the reconnaissance patrols around the small lakes. My team could rapidly find itself in the front line. The time factor is decisive. We must react without delay to the slightest initiative on the part of our target. A single small mistake and fiasco will result – and who knows when another opportunity will present itself. We check the state of our equipment and set out evacuation drills.

On the Saturday, very early in the morning, Roger, Paul, Sean and I get into our positions on the north bank of the great lake, in the middle of dense undergrowth, hidden by vegetation that goes down to the level of the water. All that remains is to embark onto the water. We spot a small, isolated track that goes down to the lake. It is covered with brambles and it takes us two hours to make our way to the bank. The place is deserted. Perfect. The mission is starting well. Team number two takes up its position south, near the small lakes. Like us, it is equipped with very sophisticated communication equipment and a boat. It is supposed to intervene only in an emergency. On his side, John, our free agent, roams the surrounding area with his magic briefcase crammed with listening equipment.

It is a beautiful day. The sun gently warms the lake; it is idyllic sailing weather. We look like peaceful holidaymakers out for a fishing trip. Little 'seals' designed to help us move through the water have been fixed to the outside of our vessel and our special equipment has been hidden among the fishing tackle. Not far from the bank, we have dropped an ambient noise buoy before letting fall our outboard motors which are now lying three yards below the surface, carefully camouflaged by a tangled mass of algae and aquatic plants. Several hours later, we return to the camp, our fishing rods prominently on show.

Midnight. The forest is sleeping. Roger and I discreetly move away while the others sit around the fire. We have put on our diving suits. After picking up our oxygen bottles, hidden in a bush near the bank, we plunge into the icy water of the lake. The equipment works perfectly. Our respirators are regular and we dive down to the algae-covered bed towards the buoy and the two 'seals'. Our diving spotlights light up the metal outlines of the two motors, which look like miniature submarines. We untie the straps keeping them in place. The engines start up first time, the 'seals' begin working and we start training. My lips are burning. An unpleasant feeling in contact with the icy water. But soon I no longer feel anything. Neither cold nor pain. I suppress a rising panic. Above all, I must breathe regularly. I don't have time to worry. I concentrate my efforts on handling the seal, careful not to lose sight of the fluorescent mark that I can make out at the end of Roger's flippers, ahead of me. Our reconnaissance work has begun.

After a quarter of an hour, Roger changes direction. He veers 90 degrees left and then, five minutes later, left again, executing the diving square, as planned. After another five minutes, another turn, to complete the square within the deadline. We get our bearings from an electronic signal that marks the end point. The dive has lasted about an hour and everything has gone without problems. Several hundred metres away on the surface we see the outline of a mass of branches and brambles. Underneath, a vessel; on board, Sean and Paul are waiting for us. When we get to the boat, we dive down and place our equipment on its bed of algae at the bottom of the lake, then attach it carefully and rejoin our comrades. As quickly as we can, we divest ourselves of our diving suits and, teeth chattering, put on warm clothes. We are in the middle of December and it is icy cold. We spend the night in the middle of the brambles on the bank of the river, in our tents specially designed for extreme cold and snowstorms, curled up in our cold weather sleeping bags. We are ready to act at any moment.

In the morning, there is pale sunshine and Sean, who has been on guard duty, announces cheerfully, imitating a waiter with ringing tones: 'Room service, good morning!' He comes over, bearing coffee on a tray. A cup of hot liquid in hand, we contemplate a winter scene worthy of a picture postcard: the black, tomb-like water of the lake, bordered by the wild forest. An idyllic place for the most dangerous kind of hunting – in which the prey is a man. Afterwards, we christen this place the 'bay of pigs'. The idea was John's, a man with a black sense of humour: since the CIA's failure in Cuba in the 1960s, one would have thought the place name taboo, at least for the Agency. This time at any rate, there is no question of a fiasco.

*

The throbbing of the motor fills the air as our outboard jumps across the waters of the lake and speeds along the banks. Sean is piloting; I am next to him. Fascinated, I follow the movements of Paul who, in our wake, is giving us a demonstration of his water-skiing skills. Our outing has a double goal: to carry out a reconnaissance tour but also to show ourselves to be what we are not: happy holidaymakers, noisy, friendly, waving to the pleasure-trippers who are cruising the lake in their boats. An hour later, we are back at the 'bay of pigs' and it is my turn to put on the water-skis. My pathetic performance is topped by a soaring leap followed by a spectacular crash into the water. Sean, doubled up with laughter, nonetheless deigns to fish me out. I resolve there and then to give up water-skiing for good, out of respect for the sport and compassion for myself.

Once aboard, I scrutinise the surroundings.

The lake is deserted.

No trace of Dr Death.

## CHAPTER 4
# THE AMBUSH

WE ARE RETURNING TO THE BAY OF PIGS. SUDDENLY, ONE OF THE OUTBOARD MOTORS CRACKLES STRANGELY, THEN EXPLODES, PIECES FLYING EVERYWHERE. The control lever hits me full in the face. At that moment, anaesthetised by the shock, I feel no pain; but judging by the amount of blood flowing from my left eye, I am seriously hurt. Then everything goes black. I can't see anything any more. Blood, hot and sticky, gushes from my wound, soaking my face and clothes. I am terrified by the idea that I might go blind. Paul and Sean rush over to me. Back on land, my friends lay me down at the back of our four-wheel drive. They cover my eyes with a large bandage which is immediately stained with blood. Paul gets behind the steering wheel and lurches off. Direction: the nearest hospital.

# THE SECRET EXECUTIONERS

Jane, a renowned New York doctor, sends an ambulance from Bellevue hospital in Manhattan to have me examined by a specialist whom she knows personally. The doctor tells me I have had a narrow escape: the wound is superficial, and only some tissue and blood vessels have been affected. The lever that hit me very nearly perforated my eye as far as the brain. The eyeball took the principal shock and a fatal blow was avoided. A tremor of anxiety runs through me. I remember the premonitions I had before phoning Jo. It is as if a prophecy has just been fulfilled.

In the afternoon, I am allowed to leave the hospital, although the doctor urges me to rest for several days. No question of stopping while we are nearing our goal. I have only one idea in my mind: to get back to my comrades as soon as possible. I therefore immediately return to the Seven Lakes reserve. I cannot bear the idea of the operation taking place without me: I would never forgive myself. Fortunately, back at the front, all is quiet. I take advantage to rest and ease the pain that overwhelms me.

*

Two days later, we are on action stations: Harold and Rolf, two of Aribert Heim's most trusted men, are inspecting the banks of the large lake, in particular checking the places from where it is possible to launch into the water. They seem to be involved in lively discussion, then agree the best place to launch the sailboat. John does not lose sight of them for an instant and records their conversation.

# THE AMBUSH

The two men move off. There is the sound of an engine. Their four-wheel drive comes up to the bank and does a manoeuvre to allow the small sailboat they are towing to be put into the water. Ten minutes later, the two men begin their reconnaissance trip of the lake.

Rolf is an experienced sailor and Harold seems to content himself with obeying his instructions. Aboard our boat, Paul and Sean follow them from a great distance away through their binoculars. To begin with they are careful not to stray from the bank. When the sailboat starts coming in their direction, they move off towards the middle of the lake. The Nazis' boat encounters other vessels. Paul and Sean do not risk drawing attention to themselves any longer and decide to get closer. When they are within a stone's throw away, they give the Nazis a friendly wave of the hand. Harold and Rolf look at them and shrug their shoulders before moving off without demonstrating anything other than silent hostility. They have no desire for company – as they clearly demonstrate. Paul and Sean's outboard motorboat moves off rapidly towards the open water, then turns in direction of the numerous little creeks south of the big lake.

Following the manoeuvre from the bank, I am telling myself that they are getting on quite well when suddenly the radio crackles. It is John, giving a report.

'Owl One, this is Owl Two. The rat's friends have put a small motorboat on the water. Compared to it, our boat is the Sixth Fleet.'

71

Several minutes later, John adds:

'The rat is not here.'

Heim's friends' little vessel is equipped with a small Mercury motor of the kind not made any more, an ideal boat for water sports, fishing and water-skiing – for spending pleasant weekends outdoors. On board are four people, three men and a woman. Behind is a young man who is demonstrating a certain talent for water-skiing. The boat takes some speed, carries out a slalom, turns north then again changes direction, this time towards the south.

Paul slips on his protective suit, grabs his skis and slips into the water:

'It's time to greet the new arrivals.'

Sean accelerates. In his wake, Paul carries out waterski positions with great verve and then multiplies his feats. He cuts the wave, slaloms, jumps with incredible elegance. Sean pilots the motorboat at great speed towards the boat of Aribert Heim's friends. In the distance, Rolf and Harold's sailboat advances towards them. Paul's performance has not failed to attract the Germans' attention. There is applause. Surprised and somewhat flattered, Paul waves to them. Paul and Sean's noisy and friendly behaviour has succeeded in cutting through the Nazis' suspicion. Their demonstrations of sympathy allow our two comrades to get close and discreetly photograph Aribert Heim's friends, thanks to the equipment hidden on the outboard bridge.

On our return to HQ, we identify them all without difficulty, with the exception of the oldest. There follows an animated discussion, at the end of which we return to hunting through the photo albums and well-stocked portrait gallery of Nazi war criminals. Sean, who has a phenomenal memory, is convinced that he has already seen him. While we are going through our archives, he said:

'It could be Adolf Hitler's nephew, the one who lives in New York. It could be our friend William Patrick.'

Paul nevertheless says that the identification is not certain. The individual he encountered was wrapped up in a voluminous anorak and wearing a woollen hat. We are perplexed: William Patrick, who has jealously guarded his anonymity since the announcement of his enrolment in the American army during the Second World War, hasn't been previously seen with any former Nazis. During the conflict, the presence of Hitler's nephew on American soil was widely talked about, and since then he has kept a very low profile.

During the following days, the Germans come back to the lake. Always without Aribert Heim. Our motorboat regularly encounters them. Both sides greet each other. Little by little, we are becoming part of the landscape – while maintaining our distance and without too many friendly effusions. We do not lose sight of the fact that we are dealing with a group of Nazis and neo-Nazis, some of whom are present illegally in the United States. They are wary of all strangers. Which is to be expected.

\*

Aribert Heim finally makes an appearance beside the lake the following Saturday morning. Through my binoculars, I see this tall, imposing man with white hair walking towards his hosts' sailing boat, accompanied by two bodyguards. He inspects the vessel before climbing aboard. I see him smile. He seems pleased with himself. The man apparently knows how to handle a sailing boat; his movements are precise and confident. He checks that everything is in place and the equipment in good condition, then gets out and disappears into the forest.

'Shit,' murmurs Paul. 'Another lost opportunity!'

'No,' I say. 'This time, we've got him. I feel it. He is going to go sailing this afternoon. He's just come to check out the boat. To get familiar with it.'

*

The net is about to close in around Heim again; our concentration, and our nervousness, are at their height. Several hours later, Aribert Heim gets on board the white sailing boat, which then moves away from the bank, gliding silently across the calm water of the lake. He is not alone. Harold is sitting beside him. We have more trouble identifying the third man. After studying him carefully through the binoculars, Paul declares:

'It's Heinz, Marcus's son – Marcus is the rat's best friend.'

The two men were together in the SS. According to our information, Marcus has gone to ground in Venezuela.

## THE AMBUSH

Heinz is at the tiller. The boat changes direction, starting to tack towards the middle of the lake. We let it get out from the shore. When it is far enough away, we – Roger, Paul and I, armed with revolvers and pistols with tranquillising darts – start up in our turn and head towards him. Approaching at great speed, we change direction when we get to within 150 yards of the boat. Aribert Heim and his men are watching us. We wave to them with large, friendly gestures. Unlike the times before, however, their reaction is now frankly hostile: we are far from the applause that has previously greeted Paul's nautical performances. Heim shoots us a dirty look. Several minutes later, we make another run, much more slowly this time, to within less than 30 yards away. Harold gets up, goes towards the rail and, waving his enormous hands, gesticulates for us to move away. I direct my most radiant smile at Aribert Heim and give him a great, friendly wave:

'Hello, my friend; nice day!'

'Get out of here!' screams Harold, in a strong German accent.

'What? I can't hear you,' cries Paul.

Our motorboat gets a little closer still to Heim's boat. We let ourselves go, screaming at the top of our lungs:

'Hello there. Nice day. Have a good sail. Enjoy your fishing!'

On the sailing boat, the tension has reached fever pitch.

Everything then starts to happen very quickly. Heinz gets out a small transmitter from his pocket and speaks a few words, doubtless to their friends in the small motorboat that is following the shoreline. Laughing, we continue getting closer and closer. There is consternation aboard the sailing boat. Harold says something to Heim. John has warned us: beware of Harold. He is a Nazi through and through, an elderly, cunning man, suspicious by nature and above all violent: a pure product of the Third Reich. Suddenly, Harold bends down to a bag of fishing rods propped up on the bridge and gets out a hunting rifle. He doesn't take aim at us or threaten us directly but simply displays the weapon. The message is obvious. He clearly knows nothing of our intentions – otherwise he would open fire without a second's hesitation. He contents himself with this 'warning', thinking we are overly invasive holidaymakers who have to be kept at a distance. Needless to say, the message does not impress us. Aribert Heim's friends are patrolling near the bank. Suddenly, we veer into the middle of a large wave that shakes the sailing boat; the Nazis gesticulate and then grab hold of the rail to stop themselves falling into the water. Paul revs the engine up to maximum speed and the outboard jumps along the water, as though about to take off. We are making for the southern part of the lake. Once we can no longer be seen by Aribert Heim's boat, we change direction several times before returning to our hideaway on the 'bay of pigs'.

Night falls over the lake and we disappear without trace into the tangled mass of vegetation.

\*

# THE AMBUSH

Two days later, Heim is back on the shore of the big lake. He is, of course, not alone but accompanied by his hosts and his henchmen. He is in a bad mood. His gestures are jerky, he looks around furtively and is clearly worried and nervous – everything about him conveys anger. He paces up and down for half an hour before leaving with his coterie for Rudy's house. A little later he emerges, calmer, and makes for the little makeshift port, where he jumps into a small motorboat, briefcase in hand. Harold, Heinz, Rolf, one of his gorillas, and one of the children of the family join him on board. Heinz is at the tiller; as soon as they have all sat down and put on their lifebelts, the boat leaves the shore and makes for the middle of the lake, under John's surveillance.

At the other end of the lake, we are on board our motorboat. For the moment, we will not act; there are too many people on Heim's boat and we do not intend to put the little boy in danger. From time to time, our boat comes to a standstill and there is a change of skipper. Time goes by and each of the passengers takes a turn at the helm, overseeing and carrying out several changes of direction. Finally, the Nazis' boat does an about-turn and returns to the shore. Our radio crackles into life. It's John.

'Owl One, this is Owl Two. The boy, Heinz and Rolf have left the motorboat.'

Two minutes later, another message from John. The motorboat is leaving again. On board, Aribert Heim and his bodyguard and right-hand man: Harold. The Owl is unfolding its wings. The moment we have been awaiting for so long has arrived. Paul starts up our outboard motor again. The winter cold is beginning to be felt but remains bearable thanks to our special suits. The other teams of The Owl, posted all around, converge towards the great lake, following Barney's order. Each receives his instructions: above all, they must cover our team and watch all the movements around the house of the Nazis' hosts. The targeted boat is moving very slowly. Aribert Heim and Harold do not seem in a hurry. When it gets to the middle of the lake, the vessel slows down even more and then comes to a complete standstill. Hard to know whether it is a breakdown or whether the two Nazis have simply decided to stop. The boat floats, far from the bank that we can barely make out. All is calm. We stop and wait patiently, though feverish with excitement.

Suddenly there is the sound of an engine. I jump, my pulse racing; my two companions-in-arms also experience a powerful surge of adrenalin. We study the motorboat through our binoculars. Aribert Heim and Harold are in deep conversation – so their little cruise was designed to allow the two men to discuss freely, far from curious ears. They seem to be arguing. Heim opens his briefcase and gets out a large sheet of paper. Perhaps a map; impossible to say – we are too far away. Leaning over the document, the two accomplices are engaged in lively debate, but this time it is Harold who seems to be holding sway. He runs his hands all over the map, gesticulates, gets annoyed. Sitting calmly, Aribert Heim listens to him. From time to time, he also points to the map and says something. We observe the scene. We would give much to be able to see this document and listen to the conversation. Paul gives an account of the situation to Barney and to the other teams. Each holds his breath. Suddenly, we hear Barney's voice declaring in a serious tone over the radio:

'Good luck everyone.'

The tension again mounts a notch. This is the green light we have been waiting for. Roger studies the faces of his team. With a thumb sign, we let him know we are ready. We attach our belts and prepare our weapons. Roger revs the motor up to full power and our boat speeds off after our prey.

In the distance, ahead of our bow, we see the Nazis' boat. Paul, who is watching the events through his binoculars, makes out signs of fevered agitation as we get closer.

'Watch out! Harold has put something in his bag!'

We are 100 yards from our prey.

'The bastard has a rifle in his hand – Danny, be careful!'

I nod my head. I arm my M-16, ready for all eventualities. We have been expecting the Nazis to be heavily armed.

We go straight ahead on a collision course. Forty yards. Thirty yards. Aribert Heim and Harold have understood and direct frenetic gestures at us. Twenty yards. Realising their efforts are in vain, Harold brandishes his rifle and opens fire in our direction. The bullets whistle just above our heads. Harold is too nervous to take good aim. Paul and I shoot back while he reloads and again lifts the barrel of his weapon.

Hit in the chest and legs, Harold is thrown out of the boat, his rifle still in his hand. He plunges down into the water and then his body resurfaces, inert. Is he wounded or dead? No time to check.

We are ten yards away. I see Aribert Heim. He too has been hit. His face twisted with pain, he is bent over to one side, his left hand pressing against his leg. With his other hand, he is holding a pistol which is pointing at us. He does not have time to shoot. The reinforced bow of our motorboat has smashed right into the rear of his vessel with an extremely violent shock force, shattering its engine. Aribert Heim's little boat is thrown into the air, flips over, smashes against the surface of the lake, bounces and then shatters into pieces. A great spray of water spurts out, spitting out bits of wreckage all around.

At that point, Roger arrives at the collision site and slows down. We examine the floating debris without making out anything. I tell my comrades what I saw:

'He was wounded in the leg.'

'Shit,' pronounces Paul, 'I hope he hasn't drowned…'

'Yes, a quick death is much too good for him. The rat doesn't deserve such a "present".'

He is right. Our mission is to capture Dr Death alive so as to bring him before our court. If we have killed him, we have failed.

Prepared to open fire, we continue our inspection of the wreckage, listening out for the slightest sound, searching for any sign of life. In vain. All that remains of Harold is a black cap floating on the surface of the water.

# THE AMBUSH

'Heim! Aribert Heim!'

I sense our prey has escaped us; the only response is the silence of the lake. In fury, tears in my eyes, I shoot into the water until my gun is empty.

'Look! Over there!'

Roger is pointing to a dark object in the middle of the debris. It is Aribert Heim's briefcase. We hurry over to get it out and realise that its owner has had the presence of mind to close it before the shooting; its contents are intact. We hope to find in it information crucial to our organisation.

'The rat must have drowned,' says Roger in his radio report to Barney. 'There is nothing but debris left here – it's like a plane has crashed.'

'One second,' interrupts Barney. 'John tells me that an unidentified outboard motor is coming towards you. Hang up immediately.'

To our great regret, we are forced to abandon our search and leave the place, after having peppered the pieces of wreckage with a last salvo, in the unlikely event that Aribert Heim has survived. Time is on our side. If he is still alive, there is little chance that he could outlast a period, however brief, in the icy waters of the lake.

Under a darkening, grey sky, we go back to our hideout. Despite the speed of the boat, the return seems long and difficult to us. Roger takes the tiller without saying a word but his lost expression, his eyes gazing far off into the distance, betrays his disappointment. Paul has a completely helpless air.

As we move further away, I again scrutinise the water with my binoculars. Still nothing. Furious, I give a violent blow with my hand to the outside of our motor. The pain does not succeed in assuaging the feeling of regret. It will still hurt a week later...

Arriving back safely, we finally dare to look at each other, with sad, resigned expressions. I hope with all my heart, in the name of the children of the Holocaust, that God will spare Aribert Heim no suffering.

At the camp, Sean, who has been following the operation as it happened thanks to our radio, welcomes us with a large smile.

'The Nazis are all dead! Why do you look so miserable? You seem overcome. Have I missed something?'

'No, no, but Aribert Heim is dead. We won't be able to try him now.'

'And so, what's the problem?'

'We haven't even found his body.'

'You have done excellent work. He is dead, there's no doubt of that. If you want to be certain, go back to the site tomorrow morning at dawn and find the body.'

I believe I can detect a touch of irony in Sean's voice. I look at Roger. His eyes are shining. He thinks the same thing as me: excellent idea. Sean has caught on:

'Hey, guys, I was joking.'

I cut in.

'We'll go back early morning. I won't be able to do anything until I know what happened to the Nazi.'

'And Barney?'

# THE AMBUSH

'He will hardly be enthralled to know that we are going back to the site,' says Roger. 'We are aware of the risks. I know we shouldn't do it. But all the same, we'll carry out a reconnaissance dive tomorrow at dawn.'

We unload all the equipment from the boat and stow it in the boot of our gigantic Ford Blazer, then hide the outboard motor under branches and brambles. Two hours later, we go in to one of those family cottages that are the delight of holidaymakers and tourists. The rest of the organisation is waiting for us there.

As I cross the threshold, I do not expect the welcome that awaits us. Our comrades explode as soon as they see us. Hugs, kisses, slaps on the shoulder: the group showers its joy on us. I am stunned by this reaction and notice with emotion that Barney and his wife Jane are kissing each of the participants in the operation. Suzanne is also congratulating every member of the team. I interpret the beaming smile she is very pointedly giving me as the mark of a deep affection. With a light step, her arms open, she rushes over to me. We stand opposite each other, holding hands for several long minutes. Then Suzanne clasps me to her and murmurs in my ear:

'My parents would be very proud of you today.'

I will never forget that display of recognition and esteem on the part of this admirable woman who has lost her entire family in the Holocaust. These words are the payment for my work and justify all the anxiety and tension I have suffered. I remain wordless. I take her in my arms in my turn and kiss her on the cheek.

'Hey, leave us a bit!' says Paul, giving me a resounding slap on the back.

'Can't you see you're disturbing us?' Suzanne immediately replied.

Everyone bursts out laughing as she pulls Paul to her and hugs him. Barney's voice is raised up:

'Excuse me for interrupting, but we still have work to do. Let's go into the next room to have a debriefing and decide what to do next.'

*

Night has fallen over the Seven Lakes. It is cold and dark. The Rudys' residence is plunged in blackness. The armed men who have been watching over Aribert Heim have disappeared. Everything is calm. Not far away, seated in a carefully camouflaged van, listening through headphones, John is on the alert for the slightest sound, the tiniest conversation. For us it is very important to gather every scrap of information concerning the events at the lake, and above all the fate of Aribert Heim. We can count on John; if there is something to know, he will find it out. Meanwhile, in our cottage, Barney is warmly congratulating the team on the work accomplished. I find it hard to share his opinion:

'As long as the Nazi hasn't been found, we cannot close the file on the case.'

Roger and Paul nod in agreement.

# THE AMBUSH

'I think,' said Sean, 'the Nazis are already burning in hell.'

A long discussion then ensues, each one giving his or her own take of the day's events, analysing the different phases of the operation, wondering if we have made mistakes, trying to explain what happened and, above all, what we need to do now, because we do not know if Aribert Heim has come out of the confrontation alive – and, if so, where he is hiding.

'Was he able to hide behind the debris?' asks Gerald.

'Don't forget that he was shot and wounded during the attack,' I say. 'And that afterwards we shot into the lake repeatedly and riddled the debris with bullets before we left…'

Gerald does not seem convinced. I concede to him:

'You might be right. But it won't be that hard to find out the truth.'

I break off. Sensing an uneasy mood among us, I hesitate to put forward the idea of a reconnaissance dive. But Paul beats me to it and it is he who suggests that we return to the site to look for the Nazis' bodies. A heavy silence descends. Barney throws a cautious glance at Paul, who remains unflustered and repeats his argument with insistence: according to him, this dive is essential and we have no choice but to carry it out. Two camps form, in a growing tension that I have never experienced within The Owl. Roger, Gerald and I support Paul's suggestion; Sean and Harry are against – for them, the matter is beyond discussion:

'According to your description of the operation,' says Harry, 'the Nazis cannot possibly have survived. I therefore don't see why we should take the slightest risk...'

Jane and Sharon are of the same opinion: such an outing would be too dangerous and in any case this dive would not change Aribert Heim's fate in any way. Jane declares, calmly and with equanimity:

'They are all drowned. It's over.'

Until now, the nobility of our cause had sheltered us from all disagreement. Each camp is now entrenched in its own position. Impasse.

In the end, we decide to resolve the issue by a vote. For the dive: four votes. Against: four votes. Only Suzanne has not yet declared her view. Everything now depends on her. The silence that follows seems interminable to me. Suzanne looks at us each in turn – when her eyes meet mine, I think I make out a smile...

'Me too, I have fears and reservations,' she finally says. 'But we cannot leave the area without knowing whether Heim is alive or dead. We must know the truth. I am for the dive.'

I blow her a kiss of acknowledgement.

'Okay,' declares Barney, 'let's go.'

The preparations begin at once. In great haste, we draw up a plan of action and designate the team: Sean is in charge of navigation and onboard equipment; Roger, Paul and I will go to inspect the bottom of the lake. Once we have found the bodies, we will weigh them down with pieces of lead – no question of bringing up the rat's body or of leaving it to float up, and too bad for the clear waters of the biggest and deepest of the Seven Lakes.

*

Dawn breaks with a veil of fog. Our boat is anchored. A pall of damp cold stifles all sounds. Before we leave, John tells us that radio communications the previous evening spoke about a search for a boat that had disappeared in the middle of the large lake. However, the rescue workers seemed to be deliberately saying as little as possible, as though they were on their guard... John fears that they have informed the local police about the disappearance of their friends, even though some of Aribert Heim's friends are in the country illegally. Like all of us, John fears that the team will be surprised in the middle of a dive at the site where the confrontation took place, during an unexpected tour of inspection.

I feel like a burglar going back to the scene of his crime. Roger murmurs to Paul:

'We're crazy.'

Sean, at the helm, smiles mischievously:

'You see, that is what I call Jewish nerve. *Chutzpah*.'

When we judge there to be sufficient light, we take off the clothes covering our waterproof Kevlar suits, specially adapted to the water temperature, put on our flippers and our hoods, and spit into our masks before fitting them. Once in the water, we go down to the bottom in single file, along a rope that can also be used to warn us in case of danger.

After three-quarters of an hour exploring the lake's icy waters, Roger's experienced eye picks up a dark stain and he signals to us to stop – are we finally nearing our goal? He gets out his knife and swims towards his objective with all the ease of an American Marine combat swimmer. He changes direction slightly and turns around the spot. Stops. Then signals us to join him. Harold's body is lying at the bottom of the lake. His rifle is stuck in the sand, several yards away. My heart beating, I criss-cross the surroundings searching for Aribert Heim's body – in vain.

We then go back up to the surface, to rest and to consider the situation together. We have enough oxygen left for a last dive. But Roger begins to show signs of vexation and dismay:

'We will never find Heim's body. We should stop, this is madness.'

'No,' insists Paul, 'we must go on looking. If he isn't there, we must go into another area. In my view, we are more likely to find him elsewhere; I am sure that the current has carried the debris further on.'

'Impossible,' says Roger. 'I know this lake well, I dived here when I was in the Marine commandos. The currents in this region are absolutely negligible. The proof: we discovered Harold's body exactly where it should be. Just below the site where the shooting happened...'

I intervene:

'In any case, we cannot leave our boat in the middle of the lake indefinitely. We will eventually be spotted.'

# THE AMBUSH

Paul does not back down:

'A last time. Just be to sure…'

Discouraged, we give in and agree.

Day has risen over the Seven Lakes region and the fog that had protected us from curious eyes is now beginning to break up. Soon the sun will warm the atmosphere of the water surface, to the delight of the practitioners of leisure pursuits – and of Aribert Heim's men, if they are prowling the area… Nervous, certain that we would find nothing, we go back down to the depths of the lake.

# CHAPTER 5

# THE SURPRISE
# BRIEFCASE

SITTING IN THE BACK SEAT OF HIS VAN, JOHN IS WAITING, HIS LOADED WEAPON WITHIN REACH. IN THE RUDYS' HOUSE, ALL IS SILENT. THE TELEPHONE HAS NOT RUNG FOR HOURS. With an air of resignation, John contemplates a tape recorder and its despairingly immobile spools. Suddenly, he pricks up his ears; he has heard crackling. A bird call. He relaxes. It's the signal. Gerald is back. After the battle of the previous evening, the former policeman has been sent as reinforcement to back John up. Gerald has contacted his sources in the local police and the FBI to carry out a patrol around the rat's den. Gerald slips into the back of the van.

'Well?' asks John.

'Still nothing.'

Meanwhile, at the cottage, the rest of the organisation is holding a big meeting. The atmosphere is no longer cheerful and faces are tense, closed. Fatigue and defeat are visible in our expressions. Barney speaks first: a rare thing for this cultivated, refined and self-controlled man, he begins with a swear word that well expresses the disappointment we all feel.

'To sum up the situation: Aribert Heim has got away from us. The bastard has unbelievable luck. Here is the information that John has just given me: Heim has survived the attack. He was fished out of the water in a coma with three bullets in him, one in the left leg and two others in the torso, doubtless in the shoulder.'

According to the information gathered by John, Heim was saved by Rolf, the son of his best SS friend, and by two other men who were on the boat that went to his rescue. Taken rapidly to his hosts' home, he received emergency treatment from the same doctor who had seen him a few days earlier: clearly a trusted man who was fetched out in the middle of the night for an emergency.

'For the moment we have no data about Heim's health, but we know that they intend to evacuate him tomorrow.'

He is even more annoyed and saddened than us by the fact that Aribert Heim has escaped us, yet in his words there is no hint of animosity towards those who have failed. He does not criticise us, knowing that we have done our best to get our hands on Dr Death. On the other hand, he wants to understand how Heim was able to get away from us.

This is what must have happened. Wounded in the leg, Heim was thrown into the water at the moment of collision. Rising to the surface and coming back to his senses, he would have hidden behind one of the pieces of debris that were floating around. He was doubtless wounded again with two bullets when we emptied our weapons into the wreckage of his boat. He must have lost consciousness at that moment and survived thanks only to his lifebelt, which had prevented him from plunging straight down.

I refuse to accept that this bastard is not at the bottom of the lake. Who knows? Perhaps God himself ordains that death by drowning is too easy and quick for such an individual and is preparing an exit from this world for him that is tougher, filled with anxiety and suffering… I look at Roger. He lowers his eyes. We feel that we have ruined everything.

I will pursue my enemies and overtake them; nor will I turn again till they are consumed; I will smite them through that they shall not be able to rise; they shall fall under my feet. *Psalms 18, verses 38 and 39.*

For the moment, we have pursued, overtaken and consumed, but the enemy has not fallen at our feet – we have to finish the task.

Not everyone shares our gloom. Suzanne and Sean pass round doughnuts. Suddenly, Suzanne comes up behind me, puts her arms around my neck and kisses the top of my head. She leans forward and murmurs in my ear:

'Wait, you haven't seen the real surprise yet!'

I immediately turn round towards her, hoping for an explanation, but she is already at the other end of the room, from where she throws me a mischievous look with a charming smile.

The surprise? It is Aribert Heim's briefcase. The one he was clasping to him before the attack and that had been fished out of the middle of the debris floating on the lake. A standard attaché case, made of leather, equipped with two gold locks. An ordinary object. We had picked it up automatically and had not even thought to open it before passing it over to Barney the day before. But now that it is lying in front of us, the surprise is considerable. None of us could have dared hope that we would get our hands on such booty. The waterproof briefcase contains guns, bank notes, a little bag full of diamonds, and false passports. There are a huge number of notes: tens of thousands of Swiss francs, pounds sterling and Deutschmarks. In the inner compartment, a splendid Luger; the grip is made of ivory and the middle, encrusted with gold and silver, is engraved with a swastika with, underneath it, the name of the gun's owner: Aribert Heim. Beside the Luger, an Iron Cross. From an envelope made of old, creased paper, Barney takes out and displays correspondence between the Nazi and former SS men, beginning at the end of the war.

Once the briefcase is emptied of its contents, Barney examines underneath all the seams and eventually uncovers a secret compartment from which he brings out a wad of documents, among which are two plane tickets to Switzerland and a list of contacts in Switzerland and Austria – all former SS men – as well as an address book of sympathisers and friends in Quebec. As he reads the list, Barney cannot stop himself smiling. All these names, or nearly all, are known to The Owl, proof that our enquiries are well-founded. There is also a map of Alaska, details and directions to the home of friends of Heim who live in an isolated village near the lake of Karluk on Kodiak Island in the Gulf of Alaska.

Barney then gets out a report. He reads the title out loud and silence descends on the room. A dozen pages, typewritten, in German. Of all the objects contained in the briefcase, it is the most valuable. It clarifies questions that have until now been thought unanswerable, starting with the origin of Aribert Heim's current fortune.

In the winter of 1945, shortly before the defeat of Germany, heavy carts pulled by horses and bullocks rolled for two weeks through the little forest route that runs at the foot of the steep rock face bordering the banks of Lake Toplitz, in the heart of the wild region of Ausseerland in the Austrian Salzkammergut. Witnesses at the time spoke of how tense the SS were. 'One had to move quickly, the Nazis were very irritable,' recounts a local who says he saw the soldiers loading cargo onto the small boats before moving out far into the lake and throwing it all overboard.

Since then, the craziest rumours have done the rounds. It is said that trunks full of gold, silver, diamonds, jewellery and precious stones are lying at the bottom of the lake. People also talk about documents concerning the billions deposited abroad by the SS. The legend of Lake Toplitz was for many years the delight of treasure hunters who dredged up the vestiges of the Third Reich from the depths of the lake. Taking mad risks, they plunged down more than a hundred yards to drag from the sludge and aquatic plants weapons and guns, but also dozens of chests of counterfeit money and printing blocks. According to the legend, Toplitz is not the only treasure lake. But no one has ever discovered an ounce of gold or the tiniest diamond – and no document has proved the existence of treasure until now, until the discovery of this report found in Aribert Heim's briefcase. It contains valuable directions and old maps; there is mention of a lake near the small Swiss town of Glarus. We bend over a map of Austria, on which a circle has been drawn around Traunsee Lake, near the town of Abensee, sixty or so miles from Salzburg. Aribert Heim's report also mentions the mythical Nazi treasure of Lake Toplitz, but without any further details.

'There is a link between Toplitz and Heim,' says Barney. 'The chests taken from the lake relate to Operation Bernhard, the plan devised by Himmler to destabilise the British economy by flooding it with counterfeit money. In total, more than four billion false pounds sterling were printed. The counterfeiters were inmates in the concentration camp at Sachsenhausen, who were later transferred to a subsidiary camp of Guisen-Mauthausen. Aribert Heim was no longer at Mauthausen when the counterfeiters were there. But the coincidence is disturbing. And here is Heim's report referring to Lake Toplitz, where billions of pounds sterling are still lying.'

A reading of the report makes it clear that Heim had recuperated a veritable treasure 'of gold and diamonds', enclosed in three trunks – two large ones containing 350 gold bars and a third, smaller one containing 1,500 diamonds, most of them high quality ('Top Wesseltons'). Barney then came across a cloth sleeve, from which he pulled eight false passports bearing photos of Aribert Heim and Harold. Four passports each – American, Canadian, Austrian and Venezuelan – that were still current; impeccable imitations that would have allowed them to circulate throughout the world freely under various identities.

*

We sleep only a few hours that night. From now on, all our energies are concentrated on the lair where Aribert Heim is tending his wounds. We have to fight to get John to go and rest for several hours. Blessed with an incredible capacity to work 24 hours a day, he nonetheless needs to switch off from time to time. We all venerate him as a veritable electronic espionage wizard. He is The Owl's eyes and ears. We cannot run the risk of losing him and so we force him to take rest. He is temporarily replaced by Harry, our lawyer who is also a passionate devotee of electronics, and Sharon. Both of them are used to working John's ultra-sophisticated material. The other members of the group disperse into groups charged with mounting a lookout along the routes leading to the site where Aribert Heim has gone to earth, or the little neighbouring port.

All is calm. The forest slumbers, accompanied by the lullaby of chirruping birds. Our detection equipment is silent. Suddenly I prick up my ears and make out a low throbbing sound, becoming louder and louder. It is a familiar, disturbing noise and one that we all recognise. The former military men, John, Paul and me, all bristle to attention.

'It's a helicopter.'

'A Bell 206, to be precise.'

Thirty seconds later, the copter, a 'long ranger' model, indeed appears in the sky. Long and narrow, the Bell 206 is the best suited to evacuating someone sick or wounded. It passes just overhead of us, carries out a perfect curve as it loses height, then lands on a piece of ground several hundred yards from our prey's residence. Then it waits, amid the sound of the blades, ready to leave again; the pilot has not turned the engine off.

All our detection instruments have suddenly sprung into life. We hear voices over our radios, shouting orders in German. Replies ring out. Armed men run towards the helicopter. Harry informs Barney of the sudden change in the situation.

'This is what his silence has been hiding; he has really

been laughing up his sleeve at us,' Barney declares. 'We can do nothing. Stay at your post, everyone.'

A station wagon springs out of the garage and slams to a stop in front of the helicopter. Rolf and the doctor jump out. Rolf opens the rear door, leans forward to help a very sick Aribert Heim who is coming out, supporting him under the right arm; the doctor holds his patient under the other arm and helps him lie down on the rear seat of the helicopter. Rolf buckles up Heim's belt and jumps up beside him with the doctor. The door of the Bell 206 slams shut again while the engine quickly revs up to its full power.

The pilot takes off, gets altitude and speed and then, the apparatus slightly tilted to the ground, begins making off in a north-easterly direction. The whole operation has not lasted more than five minutes.

'They're going towards Hunter Mountain,' says Gerald.

'I don't think so,' I say, 'this kind of helicopter can go for up to just under 400 miles, at low altitude, at a cruising speed of 150 miles an hour. Such a range would allow Heim to be taken as far as the Canadian border.'

Anger and disappointment. We feel as though all our work has been wiped out. We had thought of everything, or almost. We have been watching over all the possible escape routes, counting on John's electronic laboratory to warn us of all suspicious movements. And here we are suddenly wrong-footed on the ground, stunned, powerless. We all watch as our prey flies away.

## CHAPTER 6

# THE BEAST'S LAIR

UNTIL THIS DAY IN SPRING 1981, 'BLACK FOREST' WAS FOR ME NOTHING MORE THAN A SICKLY CAKE. But today, catching a glimpse in the distance of the dark woods encircling the Merkur mountain, my nausea is of an altogether different kind. Indifferent to the landscape that is flashing past us beside the motorway, I declare:

'I feel like I'm in enemy territory. It's the first time I've come to Germany and I really hope it's the last!'

At the steering wheel, John bursts out laughing.

'Danny, calm down. I also don't hold a candle for the Germans, but the war is over. We are at home.'

There is a pause, then he corrects himself:

'Or almost, anyway...'

John is not altogether wrong. How else to explain the ease with which the two Americans who were waiting for us at Frankfurt airport had allowed us (more out of a desire to be discreet than to hide the compromising material) to bypass the police and customs controls? John's two friends had thought of everything. Weapons, sophisticated electronic listening equipment – everything was waiting for us at the airport exit. I refrain from asking John questions. Who are these men? CIA? DIA? NSA? It was of little importance. There are pros, whatever agency they belong to, and allies. That is all that matters.

We have gone past Karlsruhe, on our right.

'During the war,' explained one of John's friends, 'the town was entirely destroyed, while Baden-Baden was totally spared. To safeguard the victors' pleasure, say the gossips. The French occupation forces who were established in the thermal resort until the beginning of the 1970s never had cause to complain of their posting.'

We are nearing our destination. On the hillsides, vines ripening in the sunshine, we pass through wine-making villages with luxurious inns, everything smelling of choucroute, marjoram liver sausage, beer and Riesling. I do not, however, manage to absorb the charms of the region. I think of our friends who have stayed behind in the United States. Of our dismay and confusion after Aribert Heim escaped. Of the weeks and months that we have lost. Of Baden-Baden, where our long chase is currently taking us.

*

Baden-Baden had thermal cures, Belle Époque hotels, luxuriant gardens... and Nazis. What better place to hide a former dignitary of the Third Reich? Leaving behind on our right the colourful flowerbeds and fountains of Lichtentaler Allee, former meeting place of European nobility, we cross the River Oos. Two minutes later, we are going past the line of beautiful houses on Maria Victoria street. We slow down in front of number 26. On a golden plaque is inscribed the name of the owner, 'Dr Heim', followed by that of his wife.

'Incredible,' I say. 'The Butcher of Mauthausen still has his plaque, like any old doctor!'

'Gynaecologist. He practised until the beginning of the 1960s,' explained John. 'He was the darling of Baden-Baden high society. His wife Frieda is a purebred aristocrat. Very rich. They had two children. The first, Aribert Christian, lives in Heidelberg. The second, Rüdiger, lives in the house with his mother.'

'Is he still in contact with them?'

'**Not officially.** They claim to have nothing more to do with him. But in the beginning, his sister Berta Baret, carried on seeing him. Her telephone was tapped and she was watched.'

'By whom?'

'Investigators, the German police, the Israeli services, the Americans, us... Everyone who was looking for him.'

And then in 1962, after the Eichmann affair, the Germans began sweeping up their own backyard and tracking down the war criminals who were in Germany. An arrest warrant was issued against Heim. But he enjoyed strong protection. On 12 December 1962, the day before his planned arrest, he received a phone call from a friend in a very senior position, doubtless a minister in the Justice department, advising him to escape. With a simple attaché case for luggage, he climbed inside a big Mercedes and disappeared into the night. Since then, he has been everywhere and nowhere. His presence has been alerted in Spain, Switzerland, Austria, even Germany. He possessed a residential building in Berlin, from which he was still drawing income in 1978-79. Not having been officially declared dead, he continues to draw his pension. In his account in a subsidiary of the Sparkasse bank (number 0063282107) 1.2 billion dollars lies untouched.

Our American friends have done a good job. They have found us a base a stone's throw from 26, Maria Victoria Strasse. We begin surveillance of the Heim house, opting for a lightweight machinery. The house telephone is tapped and the conversations followed by satellite microphones. Soon we realise that Aribert Heim's family is plunged in torpor. Only a woman and her child live there. Taking advantage of their absence, we carry out a reconnaissance mission.

We enter the grounds, with its well-cared-for lawn, without difficulty and slip behind the trees. Coming within a few yards of the superb neo-Renaissance building, we get out our equipment and examine the front of the house closely — every window, every place that might betray the presence of our prey. Nothing. We get closer, looking in through the windows. Still nothing. A last reconnaissance, inside the house, is just as fruitless. Aribert Heim has not come here to tend his wounds.

To put our minds at rest, we stay on the lookout in Baden-Baden for a week. In vain. Waiting and tedium are part and parcel of the chase. I am used to spending days listening to or reading the account of banal, boring telephone conversations. It is with unfeigned joy that John and I leave, even though empty-handed.

*

Meanwhile, in the United States, our team has been having more luck. We had had the time to take down the licence number of the helicopter used to ship Aribert Heim out. The trail was hot and we had to move quickly. Thanks to his contacts in the central administration of Oklahoma civil aviation, Gerald had quickly obtained the name of the air company that owned the helicopter and of the aeronautical club from which it had taken off; several days later, he has the name and address of the pilot. The man agrees to speak to us in exchange for guaranteed anonymity and a considerable sum of money. He tells us that he had taken the helicopter to Massena, north of the Adirondacks, near the Canadian border.

'Did you hear what your passengers were saying?' asks Gerald.

'They were talking in German. I didn't understand anything.'

'We need all the details you can give us.'

'I was contacted by a company to go and collect four men in the Seven Lakes region. As soon as we landed, a trailer approached the helicopter and three people got out to help a man who had difficulty walking. I only understood he was hurt when I saw one of his friends, doubtless a doctor, examining him. I also remember that the wounded man groaned from time to time. It was only when they got out of the helicopter that I saw the bandages soaked with blood.'

Gerald declares: 'If you had known who it was, you would have thrown him out during the flight.'

The pilot remains silent for a moment, flabbergasted, then goes on:

'I heard one of the passengers say the word "passport" and someone else replying in German in a satisfied way: "Gut, gut, wunderbar"... When they got to their destination, the wounded man was transferred into a minivan. One of the Germans gave me a tip of 250 dollars. Then the vehicle made off towards the north. I swear that's all I know. My role was over when I landed.'

'Good. One last thing,' said Gerald in a dramatic tone. 'This whole story concerns the national security of the United States. It is classified top secret. You cannot talk about it to anyone, not even your family.'

Appalled, tears in his eyes, the pilot catches hold of Gerald's arm:

'I am real American patriot, always willing to serve my country... I hope you get your hands on these spies.'

Gerald finds it hard to keep a straight face.

*

The Owl has unfolded its wings again, even if the trail to its prey has gone cold. We fear that the Nazis have crossed the border, to go to ground in Canada. We try to gather information by looking into the only two plausible hypotheses: either they have left the United States (as most of us think) or, if they have stayed, they are hiding somewhere, doubtless in the north-east of the country. Whatever the case, a slow and laborious work of ants awaits us. As if everything we have accumulated is of no account, as if we are starting from zero. But our determination is intact.

'We will corner them and drag them before our court,' Barney says to us, 'whatever it takes to do it. Don't spare a single moment and don't worry about finances. I have put millions of dollars into this mission and if necessary I won't hesitate to double the sum.'

Everyone knows that he is not joking.

And so our investigations begin again with a vengeance. We base ourselves on the information accumulated by The Owl before the start of the mission, and on the mine of information contained in Aribert Heim's 'surprise briefcase', beginning with the names and telephone numbers in the diaries. Under

Jane's direction, Suzanne and Sharon get ready to watch hospitals, clinics, surgeons, doctors and nurses north of the airport where Heim's helicopter landed at the Canadian border. Christened the 'woman's team', the trio is reinforced by Sean and Gerald. Roger, Paul and I are in charge of exploring the Canadian territory. With the exception of Roger, all the members of the team speak good French, some fluently, which is of course a great advantage in that region. As usual, John makes up a team by himself, accounting directly to Barney. But this time his field of operation is enormous: it covers a large part of the north-east of the United States. The man from the CIA uses his portable listening laboratory whenever the other two teams need it. Harry, who has joined us, knows the region of Quebec well. A devotee of electronic espionage, he replaced John when the latter left Canada. A renowned lawyer, he is responsible for the logistical aspect of the organisation.

In spite of the meagre information we have at our disposal, we have taken the decision to undertake investigations in Canada without losing any time. We want to take advantage of the immobility forced on Aribert Heim by his state of health, convinced that Dr Death will sooner or later turn up at one of the homes of his accomplices in Canada.

In guise of cover, we have created an organisation in New York, the 'Friends of Nature', that has the goal of carrying out scientific research on rare species of birds living in the fir-tree forests of North America. We have had business cards printed, as well as a collection of 'association news bulletins' that will serve as our references.

We go to Canada separately. Harry leaves first, for Montreal, where he goes to hire cars, buy the equipment that we are going to need and find us a refuge – a house in a peaceful suburb in the west of the town: from now on, The Owl's HQ.

A week later, Roger and Paul set out from New York on a monospace loaded with apparently innocuous equipment. Weapons have been hidden inside the double chassis of the doors. An ex-Marine, Paul has more than one friend at the border post. He is also counting on his two best allies: nerve and luck. For my part, I fly to Canada. It is a cheerful Harry who greets me on the threshold of our new 'operational centre'. He gives me a great slap on the back, then fills me in on what he has been doing since his arrival. He had first furnished the house for all the members of the team, with discreet good taste; it is also equipped with a very up-to-date security and alarm system; the equipment brought by Paul and Roger will be secure. Then, Harry has made numerous purchases necessary to our mission: car chains, skis, snowshoes, chamois skin, ropes, ice-axes, crampons, camping equipment and special clothes. Finally, he has found a company that rents snowbikes that can provide us with five to nine vehicles very quickly. The Owl can leave on expedition to the Great North for several weeks.

Our fingers burnt by the way in which Aribert Heim has escaped us, we have decided to take every precaution. We have to be ready for an aerial intervention. My New Yorker friend Giora has given me the address of a little aeronautical club whose owner, Arni, can probably help us. It is Harry who goes to meet him; he is awaited with impatience.

Arni, of Israeli origin, is a nice, generous man.

'We work for a photo agency, a private company based in Israel,' Harry explains to him.

Arni replies with a wink:

'Any country would be proud to have such an agency! You are at home here.'

Harry tells him no more than the strict minimum, from which Arni deduces that we are working for the Israeli secret services. He immediately puts himself at our service; we can call on him day or night.

While waiting for the arrival of Roger and Paul, we leave on reconnaissance, to familiarise ourselves with the place and above all with the various routes to Montreal. We are preparing our escape route.

For a first stay in Canada, I am being spoilt. Montreal has put on all its Christmas finery. Night falls quickly and then the snowy streets are lit up by garlands and lights. We wander the city, which seems small to me but as electrifying as Manhattan, and exceptionally beautiful; then we leave the centre and climb up to explore the mountainous surroundings.

Back in Montreal, it is around eight o'clock when a car horn sounds. Paul and Roger have arrived. After the hugs of greeting, we unload the car away from curious eyes. The equipment brought from New York, of an unexpected quantity and quality, is placed in various hiding places set up in the house.

I turn towards Paul:

'Did everything go all right?'

'Nothing to report. A quiet journey, apart from a little puncture – nothing serious.'

'And at the border?'

'A piece of cake,' recounts Roger. 'Paul was at the steering wheel. A customs officer asked him the purpose of our trip to Canada. Paul hesitated a moment then with his usual sang froid and nerve, got a piece of paper out of his pocket and said just: "Business meeting". The customs officer saluted and, with a big smile, signalled for us to move on.'

I find it hard not to burst out laughing when Paul explains to me in an undertone that he had shown him a piece of paper with a letter heading of the White House National Security Council.

Later that evening, the telephone rings: it is Barney, asking for news. Paul replies laconically, in coded language. Satisfied, Barney declares before hanging up:

'Good luck to everyone! I hope you succeed in flushing the bird out of his nest!'

# CHAPTER 7

# 'THE FRIENDS OF NATURE'

W E ARE GREETED BY A LOW, GREY SKY. THERE IS A SMELL OF SNOW. The absence of wind makes the weather bearable. We have not slept much. We talk until the early morning, after having decided on the programme of action for the week. A hearty breakfast and we set off. Harry and Paul are criss-crossing the surroundings of the little town of St Donat, eighty miles north-east of Montreal. Their target: a large chalet at the edge of the town, in a relatively isolated position – the perfect hideaway, in the middle of an immense natural reserve of forests and lakes. The place is deserted, entirely covered in snow.

Roger and I leave to explore a terrain that stretches across 155 miles to the north and the east, concentrating ourselves on

Aribert Heim's two possible destinations in Canada, imposing houses belonging to the families of former SS dignitaries who were close to Heinrich Himmler. We know from a sure source that Heim had stayed here for several weeks. Dr Death knows the region very well; it is possible that sooner or later he will come here to hide himself away. We have given ourselves a week to accomplish our goal. We have other trails to follow if we draw a blank, starting with a farm not far from the village of St Joachim, south of Mount St Anne. But the place is too isolated for a risky convalescence; if Heim needed emergency treatment, he would have to stay near a large town.

At the edge of Montreal, our car takes the rapid road that runs north-east. Roger is driving. The trip promises to be long and monotonous. My companion talks. Above all about his past in the navy commando in Vietnam. Fascinated, I listen to the account of his war experiences. It is a great honour for me to work with Roger. This man, a bold and principled combatant, is also a formidable raconteur. Having come from very different worlds, cultures and military training, we complement each other perfectly and are inseparable friends. Immersed in an analysis of the Marines' training methods, we almost miss the exit to join Route 138 which will take us to our destination: St Anne de la Perade, a little town situated 135 miles north-east of Montreal and about 35 miles from the little settlement of Trois-Rivières, not far from the St Lawrence river. This was where some very good friends of Aribert Heim's lived.

## 'THE FRIENDS OF NATURE'

Buried under a layer of snow, St Anne could have come straight out of an old postcard. We drive slowly past the house of Heim's friends and carefully inspect the surroundings. The property is enclosed by a low iron gate that allows us to glimpse the inner courtyard. We locate the path leading up to the house; it is covered in a spotless blanket of snow. No one seems to have set foot there for at least a week. This is starting badly.

We drive to the end of the street, before turning around to park near a small public park, three houses away from our target. It seems an ideal surveillance point. The street is deserted and the place resembles the most isolated of streets in a ghost town. Well hidden, we inspect the house as well as the neighbouring residences. We consider the various possible modes of action, observing those details of the house that seem to us important, as well as the means of access. We have plenty of time. We are not expected at the hotel until the evening.

In the afternoon, a couple of elderly people stop for a moment in front of the gate. The woman looks at the house with curiosity, pointing to the entrance door, indicating something to the man accompanying her. He shrugs his shoulders and utters a few words. They go on their way and disappear into a courtyard, five houses further down.

'Doubtless friends of the inhabitants,' notes Roger, who continues to survey the surroundings with his binoculars.

No one else approaches the house until nightfall. From time to time, a car passes. Further on, on the opposite pavement, a man walks his dog. Late in the evening, we stretch our legs by walking along the icy streets of the town centre. An hour or so later, we return to our observation post. Still nothing to report. The house is plunged in darkness; in the other houses, activity can be seen – lights on, and smoke coming out of the chimneys. Our powerful binoculars take us into the neighbours' private lives. I declare to my fellow sentry guard:

'This is how one becomes a professional voyeur!'

At that moment, a female silhouette approaches the house holding an envelope in her hand, which she slips into the letter box. Just a neighbour? A friend, perhaps? An elderly couple, probably pensioners, appear at the window of the next-door house.

'We must go and see them,' I say. 'Being careful not to rouse their suspicions. We don't know what their relationship with Dr Death is.'

'I'll go to see them,' says Roger. 'As a researcher of the Friends of Nature. They seem bored. They are bound to be overjoyed to talk to someone.'

Time goes by. It is already midnight and still there is nothing. The house remains deserted. We look one last time in the direction of the letter box. Doubtless one of the neighbours is charged with regularly collecting the mail. Perhaps the old couple. Opposite live a much younger family; it is logical to imagine that Aribert Heim's friends would mix with people their own age. Cutting our hypotheses short, we start up the car and move away from the house.

## 'THE FRIENDS OF NATURE'

After a quick drink in an inhospitable local bar, which is practically empty, we go to the hotel where, because there are not enough vacancies that night, we share a room.

*

Day breaks over the town. Dull. Freezing cold. I whistle a melancholy tune. Roger, for his part, is radiantly happy as if he were beginning a day of summer holiday in Florida. Around nine o'clock, we go back to post ourselves near the house. This time we are parked at the other end of the street, to observe the house from another angle and to avoid attracting the neighbours' attention by parking in the same place. Roger turns on an ultra-sensitive microphone that he attaches to the inside of his shirt before getting out of the car, carrying a little leather suitcase. I am clutching the receiver. After twenty yards, he pretends to be retying his shoelaces, taking the opportunity to check that the listening system is functioning. He whispers:

'Can you hear me?'

'Perfectly.'

Roger goes into the courtyard of the pensioners' house. He throws a look over his shoulder and then rings the bell. Several seconds later, the owner appears. He greets the stranger very politely. Roger introduces himself:

'Hello, forgive me for bothering you, I am a member of the Friends of Nature...'

He slips a business card into the old man's hand and launches into a long speech about the important research work carried out by his organisation all over the world. Charles – as the elderly gentleman is called – is impressed; he takes Roger at his word and suspects nothing. With a sweeping gesture of the arm, he invites Roger into his house and announces to his wife that they have a very important visitor. The Canadians are renowned for their friendliness, but I had not expected such a welcome of such warmth. It has to be said that Roger is playing his part to perfection. Over a cup of tea, he gives an enthusiastic account of his organisation's activities, talking about the birds of the region with obvious passion for his subject. The illusion is astounding – and hilarious! The old couple seem fascinated by his work. Roger talks to them about the cardinal, the Canadian national bird, in which he has a close interest... Would they, by any chance, have recently glimpsed this *rare bird* in their garden or that of their neighbours? ... Alas, no, replies one of the little old people. Roger then changes the topic of conversation, expressing interest in the next-door garden, that of Heim's friends.

'Do you think your neighbours would agree to support the activities of our association?'

'Unfortunately,' replies Evelyn, Charles's wife, 'they have already been away for two weeks. They are not due back from their holiday in Europe for another month.'

My heart skips a beat when she adds:

## 'THE FRIENDS OF NATURE'

'They left in a hurry for an important family event.'

I can only guess what is going through Roger's head at that moment. Does Aribert Heim suspect that we have tracked him down again? Did his friends receive a warning phone call? Have they left to hide until things calm down?

'You can leave the leaflets here,' says Charles. 'As soon as they come back, we'll hand them on. In any case, we are looking after their mail...'

Roger redoubles his nerve. Very politely, he persuades them to go out into the back garden so that they can identify together the possible traces of the rare bird... The old couple begin to warm to the task. Under cover of an amateur ornithological expedition, Roger is looking for clues that could lead us to Heim. He uses the opportunity to check the electrical equipment and the telephone connections. I follow the scene from afar, delighted that I do not have to take part in this pantomime – I would not have been able to keep a straight face. At the end of this edifying tour, Roger takes leave of his hosts and promises to come back to see them soon. I wait for him at the street corner, just managing to control my desire to burst into guffaws of laughter. The door opens. Roger leaps inside, laughing.

'I was frightened that the old couple would ask you why you were taking such an age to examine five pathetic trees that have already lost all their leaves!'

Roger looks at me with a very eloquent expression. He takes a deep breath and explains:

'The problem, you see, is not the trees; it's finding a bird that doesn't exist anywhere in the world. Talk about a mission!'

*

The following morning, I join Roger for a hearty, Canadian-style breakfast.

'Our friends on the other side send you their greetings,' he announces to me.

Barney called him last night. There is some news. The rest of the team that stayed in the United States has finally found a trail that leads to Massena airport, north of the Adirondacks. One of the security guards at the airport saw Aribert Heim and his gang. He remembers having seen a vehicle similar to the one described to us by the helicopter pilot. A single detail is different: the number plate, an American one according to the pilot, Canadian according to the security records of Massena airport. The plate must therefore have been changed. A disturbing detail: the plate bears the identifying reference of the district of Quebec. In other words, of the region we are currently searching with a fine-tooth comb. There is therefore a strong possibility that we are on the right track.

'At this rate, I have the impression that everyone is going to turn up here,' concludes Roger.

'You are very certain of yourself. Why?'

'An impression I got when I was speaking to Barney. The

conversation was coded, but I understood that it was serious. He wants us to stay in the region until the end of the week and to continue our surveillance to root out the bird... We have to go into the house of Heim's friends to search it.'

I put forward a plan of action.

'First, let's go back to the retired couple. We should make sure that they were not hiding other information.'

'I am certain they weren't,' replied Roger.

'I'm not so sure. I have the impression they were hiding something. I don't know if you noticed but they were careful not to say too much about their neighbours. Their discretion is suspicious.'

Roger does not seem convinced but agrees that we should deepen our investigation.

'Do you think we should start bugging them?'

'The satellite dish will be enough, it is perfect for this type of situation. And with that we won't have to worry about the connection...'

We return to the house of Heim's friends. Out of concern for efficiency and discretion, we carry out just two tours of inspection of the access route. There are no signs of footsteps on the snow.

'Nothing to report. Let's go.'

We are about to leave when something grabs my attention. I could swear that I saw movement inside the house. I screw my eyes up. No, it's nothing. An optical illusion. I see a bizarre expression in Roger's eyes, as if he were going to say something but then changed his mind. We move away. Roger continues scrutinising the house window and eventually declares:

'What could that have been?'

He too obviously thought he had seen something.

'Perhaps it was just a reflection, a ray of sunlight. A curtain moving in a current of air.'

'That shadow… As if someone were observing us…'

We leave without knowing the truth – but also without our having had our last word on the subject.

We go back to the site that same evening. It is dark. The snow deadens the sound of our footsteps. We slip along silently as far as Charles and Evelyn's house. Arriving at a good distance, I get a small piece of equipment out of my bag. Four inches long and equipped with an aerial, it is a fantastic invention, developed during the Vietnam war to help commando groups uncover the crack marksmen of the Vietcong in the forest – a pulse beat detector. It can detect the presence of any living organism within a radius of around 500 yards. There is a whistling noise and a little red light comes on – we have the confirmation of Charles's presence. Then I direct the aerial towards a lighted window on the second floor, where Evelyn should be. Same cause, same effect. The apparatus is working perfectly. I hand it to Roger, who now points it towards the house of the rat's friends. Nothing. No living soul.

As a last resort, we concentrate our efforts on Charles and Evelyn's house. Roger puts the headphones on his ears and directs the satellite aerial towards the living room. After a few seconds, we are eavesdropping on the old couple's private life. Their intensive gossip does not spare any of their neighbours but does not enlighten us. Soon, we are in touch with the stories of all the people in the surrounding area, their problems, their weaknesses, their leisure interests and other details, each more uninteresting than the last. During the course of the conversation, Roger's name is mentioned. Evelyn finds him very attractive; she hopes to see this 'charming young man' again and declares passionate interest in the work of his association. Apparently, my accomplice's visit has made a great impression on the two little old people...!

'Shame that the neighbours have left,' agrees Charles, 'they would surely have been delighted to meet him.'

Electrified, we prick up our ears. Charles goes on:

'I remember one of the last conversations I had with Karl. He told me about his plans to leave for Alaska in spring, with Monika and some friends. And then they left sooner than planned...'

'Yes, I wonder what happened,' Evelyn continues. 'You remember when Monika came round unexpectedly to ask us to collect their mail until they came back? She seemed very worried... Perhaps something serious had happened to a member of the family?'

'But they didn't mention the slightest problem... I hope nothing serious happened.'

We listen attentively to their effusions of concern but they have no address or telephone number to contact their neighbours in an emergency. When all is said and done, Charles and Evelyn know almost nothing about their charming, quiet neighbours. Little do they suspect their Nazi past.

The light goes out in the sitting room. Our two little old people have gone to bed. We end our listening.

One o'clock in the morning. Time to switch to the second phase of the operation. We slip into their courtyard, behind the house, and move stealthily towards that of Karl and Monika. We deactivate the alarm system without difficulty. We have then to deal with the remaining problem of the two large locks on the door. It takes us half an hour to pick them, taking care not to be spotted and to leave no trace of our presence.

The door turns slowly on its hinges and we slip into the darkened house. I feel a strange sensation, which I try to ignore. It is not really the moment to experience regrets about all the infractions we have committed since the evening began. It is the first time I have spied on people. It is also the first time that I have entered a private property by breaking and entering. But I have only to remember the objective of my mission for my scruples to evaporate. Roger also seems ill at ease but, unlike me, he is ready to ransack the house.

We carefully inspect the house, one room after the other, opening the wardrobes and trying to spot, among the clothes, possible hiding places. On the walls, splendid mahogany bookcases filled with expensively bound books. An intoxicating smell of old paper and leather fills the air. Karl, the owner, could be either extremely well read or an obsessional collector uninterested in reading. A cultivated, civilised man could be an infamous Nazi, I realise, but I cannot bear the idea...

We examine all the books systematically. After an hour or so, we finally come across a secret compartment. Behind one of the shelves is a revolving cupboard. In it we find an old metal box, closed with a heavy lock that we do not have any trouble in picking. Inside are papers about Karl's past and photos of him in SS uniform surrounded by friends, some of whom are already known to us. We seize the documents, before putting the rest back in their place.

On the kitchen counter is a telephone and an answering machine; we press the button and listen to the recorded messages.

A female voice. She seems panic-stricken.

'Karl, Monika, hello, it's Elsa. Kalinki is ill; he's in a very bad condition. He is at Joachim's and wants to see you. Karluk and Larsen will also come. Goodbye.'

'*Alleluia!*' breathes Roger.

My heart pounds wildly.

*Kalinki.* Aribert Heim's nickname.

We listen again to Elsa's message, which I write down word for word.

'It's a coded message,' says Roger, 'no doubt about it.'

But despite ransacking our brains, no 'Joachim', 'Karluk' or 'Larsen' figures in our files. And yet these names seem familiar to us. We have already heard them.

'Shit!' exclaims Roger, 'I think I've got it!'

These are not the names of individuals but of the little towns where Aribert Heim's close friends live: St Joachim, in the north-east of Canada, near the winter sports resort of St Anne; Karluk, on the west bank of Kodiak Island in the Gulf of Alaska, is where Ruda and Gunther live, old SS companions of Heim; finally, Larsen is a town that gives its name to the magnificent natural reserve of Kodiak Island. There, in the middle of the forest that covers the banks of the gulf, live Dino and his wife Sophie, two more Nazis. They all have in common the fact that they served in the SS with Aribert Heim during the war and are all bound to each other by an indestructible friendship forged by the Holocaust.

The other messages are also coded. We recognise the names of places in Indian dialect: the town of Chicoutimi, Lake St John, Tadoussac, a port at the entrance to the large fjord. This is the itinerary of an escape route in a wooded, unhabited region, north of Lake St John, which we will subsequently trace by studying our maps.

We take the answerphone and put away our equipment. Mission accomplished. A last look around to make sure that we have left nothing compromising behind us. Roger inspects the deserted street before slipping outside and we noiselessly leave this peaceful district that we will never see again. The night has lifted and we make out the first light of a promising new dawn...

## CHAPTER 8

# OPERATION CANADA

Roger has parked the car in front of the public telephone in the town centre from which we usually contact our American friends. He dials Barney's number.

'The bird has made its nest in St Joachim,' says Roger.

'Yes, we've known that since last night,' cuts in Barney. 'We were waiting for your phone call to tell you about it. All the ornithologists are arriving tonight for a seminar in Montreal and we'd be glad to have you with us...'

Back at the hotel, we hungrily swallow a hearty breakfast and Roger, inveterate raconteur, launches into one of his epic recitals. But this time, instead of memories of the Marines, he confides the tragic stories of the principal members of The Owl and of their families who were decimated during the Holocaust.

# THE SECRET EXECUTIONERS

Roger is The Owl's memory and historian. I am very conscious of the honour he is doing me by revealing some of our members' most intimate secrets. I see in it one more proof of a friendship that promises to be a staunch one. Stupefied by the amount of information that he is handing me, I realise how little I know my comrades. Roger speaks of each one as though he or she was a member of his family. His attitude to Barney is one of deep reverence.

He tells me that Barney is one of the richest men in the United States. Alaskan petrol has given him entrance to the very exclusive club of the 100 foremost multimillionaires in America. Yet nothing in his behaviour betrays his social rank. Who would guess that behind this inoffensive man jogging regularly along the paths of Central Park is hidden one of the richest men in the world? And who would imagine that he is at the head of a secret organisation charged with tracking down the Nazis who have taken refuge in North America? The budget he has put at the disposal of The Owl is on a par with his fortune and his expectations: unlimited.

Roger gives a restrained account of the tragedy that overtook Barney's family. Our boss survived the hell of the concentration camps only by a miracle. He was among the human guinea pigs on whom the mad doctors of the Nazi regime carried out all sorts of experiments. He came through it alive but unable to father children; that is why he chose to finance numerous organisations assisting children throughout the world. His goal: to ensure that these children have a future so that they never undergo any of the suffering he himself endured.

His wife Jane's family experienced the same fate: some of her relatives were deported to Auschwitz, others to Buchenwald. An uncle, arrested by the Gestapo and accused of having acted against the interests of the Third Reich, was thrown from a plane flying over the Atlantic. The grandfather, who witnessed the arrest, was executed by a bullet in the head and his body thrown to the dogs. The others died in the crematorium ovens.

The trip to Montreal is one of the most painful I have ever experienced. Roger's account plunges me into the heart of the horror of the Holocaust; I listen to it with tears in my eyes. I realise that a particular fate seems to link the various characters of the story. It is natural that, in several periods of history, destiny should unite a little group of people of this sort, driven by the same thirst to avenge, in however small a way, the atrocities of which their families were victims.

The gloomy sky, the snow that falls non-stop, more and more thickly, the fog that slowly covers the route, all feed my melancholy and my anger. When we arrive in the outskirts of the city, the fog disperses; before us is presented the wintry, dismal landscape of Montreal. But the dull weather cannot dampen the effusiveness of the whole group's meeting up again in our headquarters. Barney and Jane, Gerald, John, Sharon welcome us with radiant smiles, congratulate us and clasp us in their arms.

'Fantastic work!' exclaims Barney. 'Well done!'

'I've heard about your exploits,' adds John. 'Congratulations on the answerphone coup! I still can't believe they could leave such a compromising message. This time, I am sure we are going to get him. The man hunt begins again!'

I ask for news of Paul and Harry, who left on mission at the same time as us. I do not see them anywhere.

'They didn't find anything in St Donat,' Barney tells us. 'The house they were responsible for watching has been having cleaning work done to it for several weeks and it will continue for a long time yet, according to what the workers told them. The building overseer even talked about the house possibly being sold once it is renovated. There is no way it could serve as refuge for Aribert Heim and his gang. I immediately sent them to St Joachim with Suzanne and Sean, to evaluate the situation on the ground.'

Barney sums up in detail the events of these past few weeks, then John presents us with the sum total of the information he has succeeded in intercepting with his electronic material: he has managed to establish that Heim and his men have already arrived in St Joachim – which corroborates perfectly the information we procured during our nocturnal break-in. We review the situation, envisage all the possible scenarios and draw up several plans of action. It is midnight. We take leave of each other exhausted, conscious that most of the work remains to be done.

The whole team is to go to St Joachim, where our reconnaissance unit is currently preparing the ground. This necessitates intense organisation and everyone goes to work. Harry and Suzanne take responsibility for finding a destination for the team and of hiring the vehicles we will need. Charged for my part with finding a plane and a helicopter, I contact Arni, Giora's Israeli friend. I remind him of his stated desire to help us. It is time to move from words to action. Delighted finally to have the opportunity to take part in the 'national effort', he immediately makes the necessary arrangements to put at our disposal a Bell 206 helicopter and a light single-engined plane adapted to snow landings.

No need of a pilot: practically all the members of The Owl know how to pilot a plane. The payment is made in cash, in advance. Barney adds 500 dollars for Arni:

'For all the trouble he has gone to.'

'Or for the problems he risks having,' adds John.

The light aeroplane is to carry equipment and passengers. We can also make use of it to carry out reconnaissance flights. The helicopter might be used for tailing but also in a surprise attack. I inspect the apparatus: it is not totally geared to this kind of mission. We must take it to Toronto to carry out small modifications. As I settle myself in front of the controls of the Bell 206 two days later, I am also thinking about seeing Jo again...

Barney has decided to join us at the last moment; he is sitting behind, plunged in his thoughts. John, seated beside me, has put his headphones over his ears and switched on the radio; he begins playing with the buttons. He seems to have given himself the mission of fighting the enemy in the Canadian skies. He calls to all the planes that come within our range. The voice of one man he speaks to is familiar – a good friend of his from the past. The radiophonic storm that follows the reunion of two former brothers in arms lasts a good quarter of an hour…

At the heliport of Centre Island, a little island situated south-west of Toronto's business centre, three men are waiting for us.

'This is Jerry,' says Barney, taking hold of an elegant-looking man in a warm embrace.

Jerry is one of Barney's associates and one of his most trusted men. His company is charged with carrying out the modifications to adapt the helicopter to tailing and surprise attacks. The helicopter is towed inside a hangar where the technical modifications will be carried out, away from prying eyes. Jerry's men are to install aerial photography equipment on it, including a camera, and fit a winch geared to air rescue. We fix an appointment in two days' time to collect the helicopter.

Once we are settled in the Royal York hotel, in the middle of the lower part of the town, we split up. Barney takes advantage of being in Toronto by going to business meetings and dining with Jerry. John goes to visit family whom he has not seen in a long time. My heart beating, I call Jo. We haven't seen each other for several months. Would our relationship survive the distance and my secret activities? A quarter of an hour later, I arrive at her home, race up the stairs four at a time and, a few seconds later, there I am in front of her. She is more beautiful than ever. My expression gives me away and provokes that disarming smile of hers that I will always cherish. There was a meaningful silence. Very different from the silence of waiting in ambush...

*

The following day, a meeting at the heliport of Centre Island. Present are all the members of the team involved in the installation of the new equipment, presented to us by the technicians with explanations of how to use it. All this technology is very impressive and will give us a hell of an advantage... Despite the lateness of the hour, we go to celebrate it in a pub in town. It is Jerry's treat. Our links with his team tighten a little more, something that would subsequently be very important for The Owl.

Back at the hotel, I collapse onto my bed, exhausted. It seems to me that I have just got off to sleep when the telephone rings.

'Captain Schultz, we are leaving in an hour for the airport!' John's cheerful voice rings out. 'We're meeting for breakfast in ten minutes.'

When I join my friends in the hotel restaurant, I learn that the return flight to Montreal has been delayed, after a breakdown in the equipment's electrical control system.

'It will all be repaired by noon,' Barney tells us, unhappy and disappointed at this unforeseen delay, 'but we are short of two pieces that we had to order urgently and which won't arrive until the evening. They'll be installed during the night; we can leave tomorrow morning.'

We go to the heliport on board Jerry's yacht. When we see the damage to the copter, Barney moves off to make a telephone call, returning several minutes later with a preoccupied air. Things seem to be happening in St Joachim. Our reconnaissance team has observed intense activity around the house of Aribert Heim's friends and we might have to make a sudden move. The Owl seems likely to need all its fledglings soon, ready in battle order.

Immersed in checking the functioning of the helicopter and the equipment, I do not immediately notice that Barney and Jerry have disappeared.

'Hey, where's Barney gone?'

John replies in an evasive tone:

'He's in his office, looking after his affairs and is plotting something.'

I try to drag more information out of him – in vain. My curiosity aroused, I have the feeling I'm the witness to something that is escaping me; powerless to do anything whatever, I feign indifference, wondering if the secret meeting between Barney and Jerry has anything to do with The Owl.

After two hours of various checks, reassured about the state of our helicopter – several parts have had to be changed to resolve the problem – we all leave to our different destinations: free time until the celebration dinner organised in honour of our departure. I meet Jo at the top of the famous CN tower. Through the large glass walls, she shows me round the town. Towards the south-east, I can make out Centre Island. Some helicopters land, others take off. We can see the hangar where our helicopter is waiting. I am dying to tell Jo what we are up to, to reveal the existence of The Owl. But something stops me. As always during our meetings, I feel helpless and torn. I have trouble accepting my double existence. My life is split between my love for Jo and my hatred of the Nazis. But I have only to think of Aribert Heim to find the strength to tear myself away from the only sane and positive elements in my life and return to the secret world of nocturnal birds of prey.

*

Jerry arrives at the hotel just in time. Our team is gathered in the lobby – but Barney is absent for the roll-call.

'He left the hotel earlier to go to a business meeting,' John explains to me. 'He'll join us later for dinner.'

A little voice deep inside tells me that something is going on. We will see. Patience.

Arriving at the restaurant, I realise that my intuition was well founded. A radiant Barney is waiting for us, seated next to Arni. Surprised, I wonder what our Montreal friend is doing there. Why has he left his beloved aviation club to take part in our celebration dinner? He is in the place of honour. In front of him lies a leather briefcase full of documents. Inside, I spot the transparent sleeve containing the helicopter papers. I ask John what it's all about.

'No idea. Barney's scheming...'

While I am racking my brains trying to imagine what Barney is hatching, a waiter ceremoniously brings two bottles of vintage champagne over to us. What is going on? Why is Arni there? Why are we cracking open bottles of champagne? The corks pop. Barney, beside himself with joy, is preparing to make an announcement. First of all he makes a toast and asks us to drink to the accomplishment of the mission. After having congratulated Jerry as well as his team for the serious, dedicated work they have put in, he takes hold of the documents, gets up solemnly from his chair and announces:

'I have just acquired the helicopter for my petrol company in Alaska.'

With a big smile, he comes over to me and hands me the plastic envelope with a theatrical gesture:

'This ought to interest you. From today, this little plaything is under your responsibility.'

He gives me a big, friendly shove. I inspect the documents, unable to believe my eyes. These are transfer of ownership papers, the sale and purchase agreement of the Bell 206. I feel like a child who has just been given a sophisticated toy that he has been dreaming about for a long time. At last, I understand the cause of Barney's frequent absences and the hours he has spent on the telephone. The team has just received a priceless, altogether extraordinary gift: we are now free to install all the equipment on the helicopter that will help us in our mission, without having to obtain the owners' permission.

The splendid dinner comes to an end relatively early. The parts that the technicians were impatiently waiting for arrive late in the evening, by FedEx. We are supposed to return to Montreal the following day at noon. The weather forecast is a bit worrying: it talks about a cold wave and a zone of low pressure moving towards the region, as well as a lot of snow to come. Several other meteorological surprises might also be in store. It is therefore important to stick to the planned time so as not to encounter additional problems.

The race against time begins.

We had to leave the Toronto region for the east by the beginning of the afternoon at the latest. Around 11 o'clock in the morning, the repairs are complete and the equipment installed on the helicopter.

Jerry's team tows the helicopter outside the hangar while John and I finish setting down the flight plan. We consult the latest weather forecast and take leave of Jerry, who presents me with an elegant flight journal, with a moving dedication: 'And you shall walk with God, and fly with angels.'

The engine is switched on; last series of checks – everything seems to work perfectly and the instruments react correctly. The propellers pick up speed and the throbbing of the 420 horsepower Elison engine intensifies. The moment for take-off is here. I put the radio contact headphones on my ears and look threateningly at John, who has just regulated the transmitting system. He immediately understands the meaning of my glance, bursts out laughing, turns to Barney seated behind and announces:

'Okay, okay! No fooling around on the air waves this time, promise!'

Everything functions perfectly. The apparatus takes off slowly, skimming ten yards above the ground. I execute two complete circles (what is called in the jargon 'an Indian dance') to salute our comrades who have remained on the ground, then go straight up, in a north-easterly direction, leaving the city of Toronto behind us and, with it, all the memories and experiences of these past few days. With a tightening of the heart, I think of Jo.

The atmospheric conditions get worse. Prolonged gusts of wind shake the helicopter. I study the horizon, attentive, concentrated, ready for all eventualities. After two hours of particularly arduous flying, The Owl is returning to the nest with its new weapons. We are approaching Montreal; visibility improves and I decelerate. We are flying over a motorway. John seizes the opportunity to try out our new photo equipment, pointing his lens at a car speeding towards Montreal. We are staggered by the quality of the images that are immediately displayed on the control screen of the helicopter. The equipment seems fantastic; behind us, Barney gives cries of enthusiasm, delighted by his investment. Five minutes later, we touch down at St Hubert airport, where Roger is waiting for us. No time to lose, we cover the apparatus with a protective sheet – against bad weather and, above all, prying eyes – then take the road to Montreal. Roger informs us of developments in the situation:

'The St Joachim group has told us about a significant and interesting agitation. According to their descriptions, something serious is happening down there...'

Gerald, Jane and Sharon have left for Quebec to back up the team already on the ground. They have hired a well-equipped caravan, which quickly and temporarily solves the accommodation problem. At Barney's request, Harry has rented a yacht which will serve as our headquarters and strengthen our operational capacity. The boat is anchored in the port of Quebec, ready to depart.

*

The apartment that serves as our headquarters in Montreal is deserted and silent. I have a single desire: to pack up all the equipment and join the rest of the team on the ground. But the weather has other plans. The snowstorm is so intense that all helicopters and small planes are grounded. We need to wait another three days before we can leave. At the airport, all the planes are covered with snow and have taken on strange, unpredictable shapes; from a distance, our helicopter looks like a kind of prehistoric camel.

A calm flight of half an hour has us flying over the St

Lawrence river again, to the little town of St Augustin, near Quebec. For the first time since the beginning of the mission, no one is waiting for us when we land: every other member of the team is at their post, carrying out their task. Greeting ceremonies will be for another time. John gets behind the wheel of the hired monospace while Barney acts as co-pilot. I am surprised to see that he knows Quebec like the back of his hand. It is clearly not his first stay here; he seems to have a map of the whole city in his head.

'Where is it, your hotel?' asks John.

'Don't worry, it's a charming little hotel in a calm, pleasant area. You'll like it a lot,' he added with a very meaningful smile.

Route 175 leads to the western extremes of the old area of Quebec. Barney guides John through the maze of one-way streets. A splendid edifice suddenly rises up in front of us, crowned with towers and resembling a medieval fortified castle.

'From today and for a week, this castle is your house. Welcome to the Frontenac Castle hotel!' declares Barney.

In the rear-view mirror, I exchange bewildered glances with John. Built in 1893, Frontenac Castle is a veritable jewel. In the lobby, an army of valets put themselves at our service. Recognising Barney, the porter informs the director of the hotel of the arrival of this notable guest. Soon, all the staff and management of the hotel are surrounding him and enthusiastically shaking his hand. He receives the attention usually reserved for foreign royalty – all that is missing are trumpets and court attendants...

The hotel is situated on a cliff overhanging the south-east of the old city. I have one of the most beautiful suites. Behind the curtains is a breathtaking view; I have the impression that I am at the top of the world. Below us, big blocks of ice float on the frozen waters of the St Lawrence, drifting towards the east where they will be melted by the relatively warm Atlantic Ocean in the canal that separates Orleans Island and the continent. I note with interest the phenomenon that it is in fact possible to move out of here, on board a boat travelling eastwards.

A quarter of an hour later, everyone is gathered at the port. Suzanne and Harry proudly present us with the yacht they have hired; they have converted the little kitchen into a bar worthy of the best establishments in Quebec and have also not neglected the provisioning; there's enough to take on a round the world trip. Of all the available yachts, Harry has chosen the best and the most beautiful. It is an eight-metre boat, which can accommodate from four to eight passengers. Every object has found its place on board, including the voluminous equipment brought by the team. Everything has disappeared into discreet compartments. The dining area has been taken over by the leadership. We bend over the maps spread across the table. With his finger, Barney traces the river, goes over Mount St Anne and comes back to St Joachim then opposite, onto Orleans Island.

'It's a tiny island,' he explains to us. 'Harry has rented an isolated little house there. It's the ideal location for directing the operation against Heim.'

John sets out a plan of action for us:

'The game is wounded and knows he is being hunted. He has gone to earth somewhere near St Joachim. All his faithful team are doubtless around him. Thanks to Roger and Danny, we know that Karl and Monika left home in a panic after having received a message of distress. Two other Nazis, Dino and Gunther, have suddenly disappeared from the Alaskan coast. The network that protects Aribert Heim has gone into action. These are fanatics who obey him blindly, always ready to help each other and capable of dropping everything for the cause.'

Our task will not be easy. We are no longer dealing with a single man but with a formidable, perfectly structured secret organisation. First of all, we need to gather as much information and as many clues as possible. Then, find the most efficient means of blocking all our prey's escape routes. In case of problems, they will doubtless try to flee towards the innumerable lakes north of St Joachim and St Anne. Our mission will then become impossible.

We decide to regroup our energies on the isolated point in the north-east of Orleans island on the St Lawrence. From there, we will be able immediately to deal with all eventualities. We decide to bring the helicopter onto the island and to use our Friends of Nature association as cover, using research of endangered species of birds as a means of obtaining permission to fly over the island, including at night, if necessary.

Several days later, the weather conditions improve. Harry

and Suzanne seize the opportunity to carry out a reconnaissance cruise aboard the yacht. They sail along the St Joachim coast, identifying the best landing sites, then go back up towards the north-eastern tip of Orleans Island, inspecting the territory on the shore opposite the little town of St Francis. At the same moment, John and I admire the slender architecture of the suspended bridge that leads to our destination: Orleans Island.

# CHAPTER 9

# THE ISLAND
# SORCERERS

Twenty minutes after leaving Quebec, we begin the exploration of the little island — twenty-one miles long and five miles wide. Coming down from the bridge, we drive east along Royal Road, the main route that serves six villages and goes right around the island's coastline.

The landscapes are magnificent. In the foreground, the St Lawrence river moves off into the distance; to the north, St Anne de Beaupré overlooking Cape Torment, the Laurentian mountains and the Montmorency falls, to the south, the Appalachian mountains, the towns of Levis and St Romuald, as well as the archipelago of the Isle-aux-Grues, from where the river broadens as it flows towards the ocean.

Snow has buried the wild vines whose abundance inspired

Jacques Cartier to baptise the place 'Bacchus Island' – before succumbing to the attractions of politics by giving it the name it has today, a crude homage to the French royal family. But there is also, on this Orleans Island, something dark that earned it the name given by the Native Americans – Ouindigo, the 'bewitched place' in Algonquin. When I learn that the islanders are, even today, nicknamed the 'Island sorcerers', I cannot help smiling. We are going to bring our own touch of sorcery to this place which, until now, has known nothing more disturbing than several will-o'-the-wisps after nightfall.

We see that a bridge of ice allows snowbikes to cross to the continent. We study the north bank of the St Lawrence through binoculars and make some notes on the state of the terrain. Invaluable data for establishing the mission's plan of action. Above all, we examine the slope that leads to the bank, checking the presence of farms in the surrounding area and exploring the little creeks. Our report has also to take account of the amount of accumulated snow. The river is not completely frozen. Here and there, we see blocks of ice drifting down, but it is still possible to navigate. We pass through charming villages where the first settlers from regions of France came to live in the 17th and 18th centuries, for example St Famille and St François: two sleepy towns that seem to have come right out of a photo album depicting glorious Normandy landscapes. We linger to look at several of the 600 buildings classified by the Quebec government, including the oldest church in New France, and discover to our surprise that certain bakeries dating from the 18th and 19th centuries are still active.

A paved, well-tended road takes us to an isolated house in front of which a huge, verdant courtyard stretches out. The old, two-storey 18th century building seems very well maintained. The bare stone walls and the solid wood beams combine with a harmony that is untouched by time. At first view, I am seduced by this pastoral home. The courtyard goes right down to the river; a little paved pathway runs to a pretty creek, hidden by an abundance of vegetation, which serves as a private beach. A narrow wooden jetty built for the tides allows easy access to the yacht, which will anchor there once the fledglings of The Owl are settled in their new nest.

We examine the house from top to bottom, noting all the nooks and crannies that could serve as hiding places for weapons. Then we draw up a list of purchases to make: provisions for several months, aviation articles and, in particular, signalling equipment that will allow us to improvise a landing runway that can be used both day and night.

Won over by our new retreat, I solemnly announce to John:

'I am settling here. It's the last stop on the journey. No question of going back to Quebec.'

He doesn't seem quite so ready to give up the royal suite in the luxurious Frontenac Castle.

'Take it easy, my dear chap! Don't try to put new ideas in

Barney's head. Let's be pampered a while longer at the castle. I have booked a massage for this evening. You can't be allowed to ruin everything!'

In the afternoon, we go back to Quebec, following the road that winds and twists from the south of the island to the western tip, towards St Petronille, where we stop for a moment. From the top of the bridge, we try to spot the yacht, but without success. Our comrades are doubtless sailing north of St Joachim. The biting cold attacks our faces and tears us away from contemplating the Montmorency falls, on the other side of the St Lawrence river.

Back at the hotel, a message from Barney is waiting for us: rendezvous in his room that evening, at 10 o'clock, for a reunion dinner in our honour. Beforehand, I commit the flagrant error of going to the massage session that John has booked for me. He has promised me 'an incredible Quebecker woman' and he has not lied... It was my mistake to have expected a Miss Universe – in fact, I encounter King Kong. I have no time, however, to protest or to curse John for the colossus – going by the name of Odette, with reedy voice and the hands of a butcher – pins me to the massage table and sets to. At 10 o'clock, aching all over, I meet up with my companions, giving nothing away; I am determined not to give John that satisfaction.

The dinner that Barney has organised in our honour is a marvel of refinement. As soon as it is over, we watch the film made by Harry during his sail down the St Lawrence, along the banks of St Joachim. The quality of the images leaves something to be desired but we manage to get a fairly good idea of the state of the terrain. The professional equipment installed on the helicopter will provide us with the additional information we need.

*

The winter seems determined not to give up an inch of ground to a mild spell. The district of Quebec is paralysed by the cold, to which we have trouble getting used. Whenever the weather conditions allow, we leave on aerial reconnaissance to the region of St Joachim, the St Anne mountain chain and its surroundings, and the eastern part of Orleans Island, notably the little town of St François.

One day, John and I go to Lesage airport, where our helicopter is waiting for us. After a solid breakfast, washed down with a black coffee strong enough to wake the dead, we jump aboard my 'plaything' – which I greet again as though it were an old friend – with a light heart and cheerful mood despite the dull sky. We take off towards the south-east and fly over the old city of Quebec. The St Lawrence winds along beneath us; not far away, like an enormous beached whale, lies Orleans Island. On our right, we catch a glimpse of the Citadel, a large military fortress, and on our left Frontenac Castle, easily recognisable from its towers. Further on is the little port where our yacht waits for us quietly, immobile among the other boats.

We patrol the length of the north bank. The town of Beaupré marks the beginning of the reconnaissance zone. Around four miles away, on the other side of the river, is the peaceful little town of St Joachim.

John starts photographing like crazy while I manoeuvre the helicopter, following his instructions or the navigation map. We are looking for access routes or possible sheltering places around St Joachim. Then we continue along the length of the coast, and almost a mile inland to the south-east, we fly over the twenty-five square miles of Tourmont park, which is almost entirely covered in snow, and then branch off towards the St Joachim lake, ten miles or so as the crow flies from the small town, in the middle of a wooded region that would be a logical refuge for our prey.

The helicopter describes two great circles in the sky above the lake. John gives me a thumbs-up sign when he has finished filming and we leave again for Mount St Anne in the west. I carry out several additional circles to allow John to photograph the mountain and the immense park, before swooping down towards the south. Destination: the house of Berti and Else, two very good friends of Aribert Heim. This is one of the possible hideouts or gathering place of the Nazis responsible for watching over the rat.

We approach St Joachim. I am on tenterhooks.

Suddenly, Roger's voice rings out over the radio transmitter: 'Hello, birds!'

The members of the team who are watching the Nazis on the

ground are greeting us. Roger's enthusiasm is contagious, while John is very excitable:

'Where are you? I don't see you...'

'You just have to look for us!'

Roger, a veritable champion survivor in hostile terrain, is without equal in his ability to hide in the forest. John, complaining and gesticulating wildly, stubbornly insists on forcing me to cross three more times for nothing. After this little interlude, we go over the region of St Joachim one last time, sweeping over the ground with our photographic equipment before veering towards the east. At around twenty-five miles from Quebec, at the crossroads of the tourist regions of the Beaupré coast and of Charlevoix, we fly over the vertiginous walls of the St Anne gorges. The place, wild and magnificent, lends itself to every challenge.

We look at each other. A devilish smile on his lips, John cries:

'Go on!'

'You're on!' I say, accelerating.

The helicopter dives right into the cliff; at the last moment, I execute a 'lift', pulling the apparatus straight up with all my force, a vertical ascent, and then making it tip up 180 degrees to turn around. John has a very stalwart spirit but at this point he is visibly pale.

'Shit,' he exclaims once the helicopter is stable again, 'you scared the life out of me, you bastard!'

These little acrobatics give us a lot of fun and distract us for a moment from the seriousness of our mission but something tells me that troubles are coming. A premonition.

We return along the length of the St Anne gorge and fly over the Seven Falls resort, a series of waterfalls. Once past the little town of St Ferreol, we return to the south, towards the eastern tip of Orleans Island. Without difficulty we identify the Nazis' house, a brownish chalet hidden among the trees.

'The ideal place to withdraw from civilisation,' comments John.

*

Back on Orleans Island, we have left in the deserted house two large travel bags full to the brim, several wooden chests containing electronic equipment and an alarm system that was particularly delicate and tricky to install. For the time being, we have decided to put things only on the ground floor; the rest of the house will await the arrival of The Owl's fledglings. John works quickly and well; his technical skills and his ingenuity take my breath away. After two hours, he comes out of the house, a remote control in his hand:

'We'll check that everything is working. You stay inside.'

I do so, not giving it a second thought. No sooner had he put his finger against the button than the siren goes off in an ear-splitting din. I feel like my ear drums are going to explode. Unable to stop the racket, I rushed to the nearest window and jumped outside, landing in the courtyard on the little snow-covered shrubs. Silence is restored. Then John's thundering laugh rings out; with his hand, he mimes the movement of a lift.

'One all – we're quits!'

*

It is already late in the afternoon when we take off towards Quebec. After several minutes, the cliff to which the town clings appears in all its glory. We fly over the Citadel at low altitude then I pull on the control lever while accelerating. The copter shoots straight up and stabilises at cruising altitude, several hundred yards higher. I take the buildings of Loual University as a landmark to direct me to the airport, where we land several minutes later.

In the lobby of the Frontenac hotel, we find Harry, Suzanne, Barney and Jane, as well as Sean, Paul and Sharon, who have just arrived back from St Joachim, where Roger and Gerald have taken over. Obviously, they say nothing about their mission: it is not the appropriate place for secret conversations. But they let drop several clues that give us to understand that the situation on the ground is desperately static.

After dinner, we go on board the yacht where we can now talk without fear of eavesdropping ears. The meeting becomes an information exchange. The teams swap all the details they have accumulated during their scouting trips. According to

Paul, the Nazis are moving as little as possible; they seem to have disappeared. Describing everything that is happening around the house that serves as headquarters to the friends of Aribert Heim, he concentrates on the movements of Elsa, the owner, who goes out only to do their shopping and to attend Sunday mass at the St Joachim church.

Elsa does her shopping according to a system, buying mainly food. A lot of food, mainly tins. But discreetly, taking care not to arouse the curiosity of shopkeepers or her acquaintances. Our friends follow her every time she goes out; she has been seen four times filling 20-litre petrol cans at the local service station. She also often visits the corner chemist, from which she emerges with large quantities of antibiotics and analgesics obtained on prescription, making us suppose that something fishy is afoot. Paul and his friends have the impression that the Nazis are preparing to change residence but despite all the electronic equipment at their disposal, they have still not managed to discover what is going on.

Sean tells us that during one of his guard duties, he saw two of the house's occupants standing at the first-floor window. Two sentries, rifle in hand, were watching. He is convinced that one of the rifles had a telescopic sight. We exchange looks, a little ill at ease. Barney begins speaking:

'Good, now John and Danny. What have you found?'

I open the screen and John starts the projector. Despite the weather conditions, the images taken from the helicopter are of excellent quality. We can clearly make out all the chosen targets. The film and Paul and Sean's account – everything fits together: we sense that something is going to happen. The obvious conclusion is that we need to take as many precautions as possible to ensure that Aribert Heim does not get past us again. First of all, finish the preparations and move in to the house on Orleans Island as quickly as possible. Then, take the helicopter there and, finally, take the yacht out of Quebec harbour and anchor it in the little sheltered creek. We should be ready for all eventualities, in case our St Joachim 'neighbours' move.

'Wait! One second, go back, there's something I want to see again.'

We are on our second viewing of the evening. Suzanne has seen something that has escaped us... I wind back.

'Yes, that's it! Stop! Look carefully, there, there's a man...'

She is right. In one of the three sequences filmed above the retreat of the rat's friends, we can clearly make out a man seated on a snowbike on a side path, immobile, as if he were trying to hide himself so as not to be seen by the helicopter. We carefully examine the other sequences filmed around the house. None of them contain any walkers. I go over the images that interest us in slow motion, stopping at length over the arrival of the snowbike. There is only one explanation for his sudden appearance: somewhere there is a tunnel through which it is possible to go from the Nazis' house to the forest, which represents a distance of several hundred yards. With the help of the map, the film and the aerial reconnaissance photos, we identify the precise place where the man was filmed. Our first objective is to find the entrance to this secret passage. If we can do so, the whole operation will be altered and we will have made enormous progress in our research. The place is an ideal one for an ambush. We decide to take the necessary measures to intercept the man on the snowbike.

'Sean and Paul, you carry out reconnaissance on the ground,' says Barney. Your mission is to find the tunnel. Danny and John will take over from you in two days.'

Then, turning to us:

'John, Danny, you don't change a winning team: you'll finish getting the house on Orleans Island ready. We might need it sooner than planned. Jane and Suzanne will give you a hand.'

A mammoth task awaits us the following day. I make five return trips in a helicopter stuffed to the brim while John transports by road the equipment that is too bulky to be carried in the air. On the ground, Jane takes receipt of the boxes of provisions. At the end of the day, all the equipment is in place but much remains to be done. We go into every nook and cranny of the house, cleaning and polishing like good, well-disciplined soldiers preparing for a military inspection. Despite the amount of work, we finish in time. In the evening, Jane goes back to town while John and I remain. From that moment, someone will always be in the HQ of The Owl.

*

Our companions who have not been on the ground join us the following evening. Frontenac Castle now seems very distant. The return to real life is almost a relief; I do not find it hard to give up these Quebecker luxuries and illusions and it is without the least regret that I return to reality on Orleans Island. The only thing I miss is the extraordinary view from the castle towers. Like me, Suzanne prefers the small farmhouse to the luxury hotel. Our already excellent relationship becomes even stronger. Working with her is a joy; there is trust between us and we understand each other with a minimum of communication. I think of her almost as a big sister.

Over the following days, the weather forces us to amend our plans. A snowstorm and an icy wind limit our visibility; we have to postpone our exploration of the terrain. Useless to try to fight against the bad weather since Aribert Heim's friends must also have had to go to ground in their house. We take the opportunity to review our plans and to watch the audiovisual material again in case a detail might have escaped us.

The storm eventually calms. Sean and Paul leave again in search of the tunnel while Suzanne and I prepare the yacht. We spend two days going through the boat top to bottom, drawing up a list of all the equipment and weapons on board. We are also in charge of communications. Every day brings us a new load of coded messages; Suzanne takes care of the radio receiver, noting the messages as they come to us and replying. Our labours over, we spend our evenings together, sitting near each other and, soothed by classical music, clink glasses and recount memories of childhood. Gentle moments of intimacy and warmth, too rare not to be tasted to the full...

On the second evening, it is late into the night when we set up the yacht alarm system. We go back to the brightly lit house. Smoke is coming out of the chimney and we hurry under the biting cold. Suzanne catches hold of my arm and winks at me.

'Thanks for these moments, Danny.'

Disconcerted and blushing, I don't know what to say. After a moment of silence, I manage to stammer:

'Thank you to you, too.'

I immediately reproach myself for having found no better response; before going back into the courtyard, I pull Suzanne to me and clasp her in my arms for a few seconds.

Jane greets us with a large smile and boiling hot coffee.

'The others won't be long,' she says.

From the start of the operation, we have regularly gathered together. A custom that fulfils three imperatives: to co-ordinate manoeuvres, review the situation and above all raise our morale. This regular return to the fold for the teams on the ground also gives them the vital opportunity to refresh their ideas and recoup their energies; the region's extreme climate makes our expeditions exhausting.

The following morning, the fledglings again disperse. Paul and I leave in our turn in search of the mysterious tunnel. We hide our snowbikes before making for the zone we are to investigate – looking, in our white suits, like two polar bears. Paul disappears into the refuge built by our friends; he is responsible for monitoring the radio, in hopes of detecting a human presence. Meanwhile, I leave on reconnaissance, wearing snowshoes; I move forward very slowly, on the lookout for the slightest sign or the smallest trace likely to lead us onto the trail of the tunnel.

When night falls, we approach the Nazis' retreat. The shutters are closed. Impossible to see anything inside. Our listening equipment records conversations without interest. Nothing indicates that they intend to move. We are overtaken by a feeling of discouragement; we have not made the slightest progress, despite the long, painful hours of ambush in the cold. I murmur to Paul, in a moment of frustration:

'Even Eskimos are better protected that we are, in their igloos!'

Taking advantage of the darkness, just before dawn, we make our way back to the forest. We are to go to ground in freezing woods for weeks to come, in extreme conditions, watching over our prey. Our suits start wearing out. The temperature falls to below thirty degrees – and with it our morale.

*

One morning, after two hours of patrolling, I come to a little hill in the forest, from where we will be able to inspect the back of Aribert Heim's friends' house. I stop in the middle of the trees and get a pair of binoculars out of my backpack, along with a telephoto lens which I fit onto a camera. The equipment is ready to use and I slip the straps around my neck. As I am moving in the snow towards the top of the hill to get a better viewing angle, I suddenly have the impression that the earth is melting beneath my feet. For a few seconds that seem to me an eternity, it is as though I have been struck down by telluric forces and my hands find nothing stable to grab onto. Then, just as suddenly, my fall ends. At the same moment, I feel a violent shaking sensation on the nape of my neck. I let myself be overtaken by a delicious feeling of drowsiness. Then, everything goes black.

I come back to my senses. How much time has gone by since I lost consciousness? No idea. I find myself in an extraordinary position: my head down and my feet in the air, my enormous backpack hanging above me from the end of my shoes. I am bathed in a soft white light that filters through the snow. I am in paradise.

The sensation of well-being does not last. A panicky fear overwhelms and paralyses me. I feel no pain. The worst has happened: I have been buried alive under the snow and no one will ever find me. After a few minutes, I get a hold of myself and am overcome by a fit of hysterical laughter that frees me of all the accumulated tension. Through the light blurred by the snow I can glimpse the branches of a tree; I take hope again. I fold myself and manage to sit up, checking the extent of the damage. I seem to be okay. Nothing broken, on first impressions. I try to get free, but my backpack falls on my head, followed by clumps of snow and bits of broken branches.

I suddenly remember that Paul is patrolling on the ground – if he has not been carried away by the avalanche, he must be wondering what has happened to me… I realise that I have not fallen into a hole; I lost my balance and tumbled down a sharp slope, carried by a fall of snow. Stuck against the tree that saved my life by stopping my fall, three or four yards from the edge of a cliff or a crater, I locate all the equipment I had with me, apart from my watch, which has disappeared under the snow. All is quiet. And now, how do I get out of here?

I am in a sort of lift shaft made of snow and ice, with the tree forming part of one of the walls. I see only one way out: to try to climb up to the top of the tree, in the hope of being able to get my bearings from that high position. To make my ascent easier, I relieve myself of my equipment, taking with me only my binoculars and the transmission set. I begin climbing, cautiously, but the tree begins moving and starts rocking like a pendulum under my weight. I give up the attempt. I have no other solution but to try to climb up the walls. The radio receiver is silent. Nothing indicates that my disappearance has been noticed. Paul must think I am still doing my rounds.

I put my backpack on and begin climbing by slithering along my stomach, clearing the snow above my head. From time to time, I grip onto a shrub or a tree trunk so as not to slip down. Breathing quickly, my muscles on the point of giving up, I dare not stop; I continue my frenetic climb by grabbing hold of whatever comes to hand. Distress and worry increase my efforts until... Finally! I see the open air and the surrounding forest. A last push, and I am saved.

Not far from where I fell, I sit down with a heavy movement. I close my eyes and remain motionless for several moments while I get my emotions under control. Then, at the agreed meeting place, I find Paul, to whom I recount my misadventure.

'That could have been really serious,' he says.

Worried by my silence, he had not been able to understand why I did not contact him and had been imagining it was a technical problem...

For his part, he had not discovered anything on his patrol round. We carry out a last reconnaissance before going to huddle in our refuge at nightfall. On the two following days, our long searches bear no fruit. The mysterious snowbike has disappeared, as if the earth has swallowed it up; the man is doubtless hidden somewhere right under our noses.

\*

The days are harsh and the nights even worse. An icy wind paralyses the whole region and provokes a fall in temperature from which even our special suits cannot protect us. Despite its resemblance to a Himalayan encampment, our shelter cannot give us enough warmth. I have trouble getting to sleep and my bladder wakes me regularly, to torment me. Shivering with cold, I have no intention of climbing out of my sleeping bag; I am therefore forced to use plastic pockets to relieve myself... As for Paul, he sleeps like a baby as though he were comfortably installed in a hotel bed; nothing seems to disturb him.

This morning, we leave our shelter at the first light of day. I am happy to get out of the place that is a nightly hell for me. My joints hurt and my muscles are working in slow motion. After half an hour of walking, out of the forest, we hear the sound of an approaching engine. Paul stops on the side of the road and signals to me to take cover. Three seconds later, we have disappeared. Crouching in the thicket, I get out the camera. The sound of the engine keeps on getting louder. Several moments later, I glimpse the outline of a snowbike coming out of a bend. Impossible to know whether it is the one we have been looking for. There is nothing to indicate that the rider is one of Aribert Heim's men. It could be any other inhabitant of the region.

The snowbike is no more than 50 yards away when I set the camera in motion. I vaguely make out the driver, without being able to identify him positively. He is an elderly man, dressed in a thermal suit, his face half hidden by large ski glasses. At regular intervals, he glances furtively towards the sledge he is dragging behind him. We stay on our stomachs a good moment longer, until the snowbike has disappeared.

'I hope he didn't spot any trace of us...'

'He didn't stop,' remarks Paul. 'I don't think he saw anything.'

We follow the tracks left by the snowbike. They take us to an exposed field; on this terrain, impossible to follow without running the risk of being unmasked. And we are not even sure of the driver's identity. We therefore stay in ambush, in case our man makes a reappearance. In the evening, we receive a message from Barney, ordering us to return to base.

*

It is still early. The island is plunged in darkness and the house is waking up. The members of The Owl work to the strictures of very unusual hours, but I love these moments – going out onto the little wooden terrace overlooking the rear courtyard, the penetrating cool of the dawn, the magical view from this island that is embraced by the powerful arms of the St Lawrence...

A few dozen yards from the terrace, the helicopter is covered with a layer of fresh snow accumulated over recent days. Lost in contemplation of the clouds, a cup of hot coffee in one hand, I do not hear Suzanne approaching. Her voice makes me jump:

'*His body is in the east and his heart in the west*,' she declares, paraphrasing a famous poem by Jehuda Halevi about European Jews who are longing for the land of Israel...

'You frightened me!'

'What's happening with Jo?' asks Suzanne, guessing my thoughts.

'I don't know, I haven't had any news of her.'

'No letter? No telephone call? Strange.'

We fall silent a moment and then I say:

'Yes, it's strange… I am here, in this romantic setting, beside a charming woman with whom I could easily fall in love, instead of which I'm dreaming of an impossible, far-away love…'

Suzanne makes no reply, tearing me from my melancholy dreaming by pulling my sleeve:

'Come on, come and help the others get breakfast ready.'

*

In the dark room at our house, Suzanne is developing our latest films. I slip into the cockpit of our helicopter to examine the electrical system; we have planned to try out the winch. Suddenly, I hear Paul calling me. Lifting my head up, I see him running towards the helicopter, an envelope in his hand.

'You will never guess who we photographed yesterday!' he cried, visibly moved as he held out the freshly developed prints.

I examine the photos and let loose a cry of astonishment. I have no trouble identifying the man in the photo: his portrait has pride of place in the 'family album' of Aribert Heim's friends and accomplices.

'It's Herbert!'

Paul does me the honour of giving me a resounding slap on the back.

'In person!'

Herbert is one of Heim's closest assistants and right-hand men. An SS man found guilty of crimes against humanity. A hunted animal, gifted with a sang-froid and remarkable cleverness that have more than once allowed him to escape justice. His presence was already being alerted in Canada at the beginning of the 1970s; at the time, The Owl narrowly missed him. He mysteriously disappeared after the group had been lying in ambush for him. Since then, The Owl had lost his trail.

Why had Herbert come out of his hole? Who had warned him and how had he arrived in Quebec without being spotted? No time to reply to these questions. We immediately inform the Californian cell of our organisation – they are dealing with his case. For our part, a meeting is called for.

'In any case, Herbert is not here by chance,' says Paul. 'He is Heim's most trusted man, his shadow and his double; the fact that he has come here is a sign. Something important is certainly going to happen.'

I remember his furtive appearance on a snowbike.

'I wonder what was in his trailer... It must have been crammed full.'

'Danny is right,' intervenes Barney, 'if we manage to find out what load Herbert was carrying, perhaps we will know more about their intentions.'

'It must have been food,' says John. 'I have the premonition that Heim and his band of Nazis are going to hide themselves somewhere else, somewhere between the lakes and forests of

North Canada. That was what I thought when I heard the message left on the answerphone in Elsa and Berti's house. In the coded phrases, I picked out the names of places: Chicoutimi, Lake St John, Tadussac, at the edge of the big fjord. A veritable escape itinerary that leads towards the Great North, at the approach to the artic circle.'

'We will reinforce the surveillance around Elsa's farm,' orders Barney. 'Tomorrow, everyone to St Joachim. Is everything ready, Danny?'

'I only have to check the safety equipment, which we'll need if ever we have to transport a prisoner or make an emergency evacuation for one of us. I need two people.'

There is a smell of action in the air. Things are finally going to happen.

# CHAPTER 10

# ELSA

Excited, brimming over with enthusiasm, Paul, Suzanne and I leave in the helicopter, going north of Mount St Anne, to train ourselves in the use of the rescue equipment. We have to check its efficiency after the technical modifications made to the electrical control system. I also want to check the functioning of the winch that will lift the rescue seat. From the rear of the helicopter, Paul lowers and lifts Suzanne, suspended on the end of a cable. Then they change roles and Paul balances on the end of the line. I want to reassure myself that the system functions directly from the pilot's cockpit; an improvement suggested by Paul in the light of his experience of air rescues in the jungles of Vietnam. We carry out first an individual rescue then one with two people:

Paul acts as rescuer and Suzanne and he are suspended on the rescue seat, pressed tightly against each other, which seems to amuse them both greatly – they appear in no hurry to get back into the helicopter.

We fly east of Mount St Anne; on the horizon, towards the west, the houses of the little town of St Joachim rise up. We would willingly have landed in front of Berti and Elsa's house to take the whole band of Nazis in one fell swoop and then throw them in the icy waters of the Hudson Gulf... In the distance, towards the south-east, Orleans Island clearly appears. Seeing the rural buildings, one gets the impression of looking at a child's drawing of a world over which time has no hold. Not a living soul; only the smoke emerging from the chimneys betrays the presence of living beings in that dead landscape with its ghost town air. The helicopter flies at low altitude, above the wooden tower that dominates the eastern extremity of the island and then turns to fly westwards again, along the river. We fly over the yacht and the wooden bridge to descend in a straight line and land near our organisation's retreat.

*

The church of St Joachim is one of the most beautiful works of ancient art in Quebec. Its silver bell, one of the oldest in the region, proclaims its presence loud and clear. I enter it this Sunday morning, along with the faithful, with the disagreeable impression that I am not altogether at home. I lift my cap and move forward with a resolute step. I know enough to be able to create the illusion, first wetting my fingers in the stoup, then making a discreet sign of the cross. I have even learnt the most important prayers by heart for the occasion. I move up the length of the nave, the remains of an earlier, 18th-century church. I am not there to admire the tabernacle, the lectern or the altar candlesticks, and even less to take communion. However, immersed in the sea of faithful, I don't have the impression of standing out. I recite the prayers with feigned devotion, get up at the right moment, and sing the responses with fervour. An attentive observer would perhaps discern the glances, albeit discreet, that I regularly direct towards the old lady sitting several rows away from me. Far from suspecting the attention of which she is the object, Elsa is intensely preoccupied with her fervently religious devotions.

I had had to battle long hours with my comrades to get them to accept my plan. Elsa is the weak link in the organisation that protects Aribert Heim; she is the only one to risk going outside the house in which the Nazis have taken refuge. I suggested concentrating our energies on her. Not without reluctance, my comrades accepted my plan.

Over the following weeks, I go more and more often to the church in St Joachim so that the parishioners in general and Elsa in particular get used to my presence. From time to time, John also attends mass although never in my company. His role is nonetheless far from secondary: he is the director of my plan. From now on, I spend most of my time tailing Elsa during her shopping expeditions for provisions in the shops or during her outings to the church of St Joachim. Certain that she is neither followed nor protected by anyone, we decide to move to action.

Elsa is examining a product on a supermarket shelf when I approach, stumble and then bump into her, knocking over her basket.

'I'm so sorry, please excuse me,' I say, bending down to pick up the products scattered over the floor.

I straighten up, again apologising. Elsa's blue, suspicious eyes tell me that the first step of the plan has worked. She has seen the little pendant that I am wearing at the end of a long chain around my neck and which has 'slipped' out of my shirt. It is a Nazi insignia which she recognised at first glance. I have spent much time rehearsing this essential phase of my plan with John. The cross must be visible without being ostentatious. At first, Elsa seems flabbergasted, but she quickly gathers herself.

'You have a beautiful cross, guard it preciously,' she said indulgently, before making off for the checkout.

'I assure you I take great care of it,' I say without hesitating, striking while the iron is hot. 'This cross is a souvenir of my father and it never leaves me.'

Elsa stops, her face flushing crimson.

'Who are you, young man?' she asks in German, hiding her emotion with difficulty.

# ELSA

'I am the son of Major Schultz.'

Elsa stares at me. I get out my wallet and show her a photo. She looks at it, stupefied. It is the photo of a man dressed in the black uniform of the SS.

'That's my father... Major Schultz.'

No one, not even a former SS man, could guess that this photo is a fake. The SS man in question is an actor and the uniform hired. The skill of a photographer friend of Barney's did the rest. The illusion is perfect.

'This photo and his Iron Cross are all that I have left of my poor father. I cherish them like treasures. He disappeared in the 1950s when I was five years old. Then my mother died. Her best friend, a Frenchwoman from Alsace, took care of me and adopted me. She took me to France. It was she who gave me the photo and the cross. She told me that my mother was never parted from it and since then it has never left me either. I have never heard of my father again.'

'He must be hiding too...' a thoughtful Elsa let slip. 'My husband was also a hero. He too suffered a lot after the war. He died in secrecy.'

'My father, your husband... yes, they were real heroes.'

My cover is simple – pointless to complicate things. We have studied the scenario carefully. John has even established a false French passport for me in the name of Schultz. Elsa hands me back the photo, takes my hand and squeezes it warmly.

'I am very proud to have met you and I hope we will see each other again,' she says, beaming. 'I go to mass every Sunday.'

'Me too! Something else we have in common... Well, in that case, see you next Sunday.'

The baptism of fire had gone well; now I would have to play things very delicately. The following Sunday, Elsa arrives at the mass as usual, takes her customary place in the front rows and starts to pray in silence. She turns round several times, shooting glances at the door, as if she were waiting for someone. She is looking for me but I am not there. John, seated at the back of the cathedral, keeps count: during the mass, Elsa turns round 22 times. The fish is biting.

The following week, I see Elsa again, at the church entrance. She is happy to see me and says in a cheerful tone:

'You were not at mass last week. You were doubtless very busy.'

'Yes, I am doing research in the region on rare species of birds; I work for the American Association of Ornithologists.'

I give a passionate exposition of the association and its activities; the more I talk, the more interest and enthusiasm she displays. This second encounter is followed by several others; each time, I let her talk as much as possible and above all avoid asking her questions.

'One of these days, we'll invite you over. There are a huge number of birds in the woods near our house, particularly in spring and summer. I am sure it will help you in your research.'

She didn't know how right she was... But I don't hold any illusions, the situation is too tense; it is not the moment for Heim's friends to have guests. But this theoretical invitation is at least proof that I have succeeded in winning Elsa's confidence. In any case, I have no intention of accepting, for obvious security reasons – we don't know what the Nazis suspect of our activities, after all. The risk of falling into a trap is much too great.

Several days later I bump into Elsa 'by accident' at the St Joachim chemist. Her sombre demeanour and extreme agitation indicate that something is wrong. She will not look me straight in the eyes and her expression has a feverish aspect. She gives me a tight little smile.

'Ah, Elsa! I'm happy to see you! How are you?'

'Not well. We have big problems at home and we have to leave for Austria.'

She is lying. Even at death's door, Aribert Heim would never take refuge in Austria, where he would risk being arrested.

'I'm really sorry... If I can help in any way, don't hesitate to ask... When are you leaving?'

'Soon, as soon as we get the necessary papers,' she explains without giving any more detail.

The following Sunday, as she is coming out after the end of mass, she bursts into sobs and tells me how difficult things have been the whole of the previous week.

'I am in danger and I cannot go on like this,' she says in a broken voice. 'We are under threat... Someone wishes us harm, but we don't know who...'

'Why don't you file a complaint?'

Silence.

'Do you want me to go with you to the police?'

'No!'

'Do you want me to go for you?'

'No, no! Absolutely not! We do not know what it's about or who is responsible. We don't want to involve the police unnecessarily.'

Touched by my concern, she has more and more trust in me.

From now on, we form the habit of meeting during the week in the imposing church of St Joachim. The place is deserted. We speak in low voices. Elsa is not sparing in her confidences, if not confessions. In me, she has found an attentive ear. She is a courageous and determined woman, with a certain resemblance to Eva Braun, Hitler's mistress. She seems constantly on the edge of a breakdown. Tense. Anxious. She speaks without stopping as if outside of our meetings she is cloistered in silence. I drink in her words, accumulating the details about the 'glorious' past of certain of her friends, principally Rolf and Herbert, with his shadowy reputation. But she never speaks about Aribert Heim...

Our encounters are followed from afar by John. As usual, he has come into the church after us, as discreetly as possible. Leaning on a pillar he photographs us – at exactly that moment, Elsa turns her gaze in his direction. Terrified, she lowers her head towards me and asks me, half hysterical:

'What is it? What's going on?'

I try to calm her down – it is doubtless just a tourist who has taken our photo completely at random... I am perturbed. In a fraction of a second, John has ruined weeks of effort. I try to save the situation:

# ELSA

'Look, he is photographing all over the church...'

John is wandering throughout the church, photographing everything he can find of interest.

'We are being followed,' murmurs Elsa, 'we must get out of here.'

We take leave of each other without saying goodbye. I will never see Elsa again. But the information I have extracted from her will prove to be extremely useful and will serve to hasten the denouement.

*

Over the following days, we reinforce the surveillance of the house, looking for any chink in the armour, assembling the various pieces of the puzzle bit by bit. We are beginning to get a view of the whole. Recently, an abnormal activity has put us on the alert. All the information we have been gathering for several weeks fits together: Aribert Heim intends to move. When? We do not know. For the time being, by remaining huddled in his lair, he has the advantage. We have to act. Quickly.

We decide to force Heim and his gang to leave their hideout as rapidly as possible, in an emergency, without giving them time to draw up escape plans. Germans are old-fashioned; they are not in the habit of moving without meticulous organisation. Forced into a corner, there is every chance they will panic and make mistakes. But they must not think we are making a head-on attack. We plan a series of serious incidents to make them

177

emerge from their den. We must take their likely reactions into account. First, they are armed and dangerous and they will not hesitate to use their weapons against us; judging by their behaviour up to now, they will not call on the forces of law and order. They will choose rather to put up physical resistance or to escape to another hideout until things calm down. Most of the Nazis surrounding Heim live in the US or Canada completely illegally. Two of them, considered war criminals, are wanted under international arrest warrants issued in Europe. We also do not forget their logistical capabilities and the varied range of hideouts at their disposal. Finally, there are many members of the band whom we have not identified. Like us, their group has access to many resources and their network has a very solid base. We cannot rule out the possibility that a large Nazi organisation, such as 'Der Spinner' or 'Odessa', is helping Aribert Heim and lending support in case of need. We know that these secret organisations, created just after the war and equipped with huge resources, are still operational in Europe, the USA, Canada and Latin America.

Our meetings are feverish. Our eyes shining, we are seized with enthusiasm as we draw up our plans. The team splits into little groups of action: two groups of two people are responsible for attacking precise targets, while the rest of the team is deployed around the property, ready to intervene in an emergency.

The hour of action is here.

# CHAPTER 11
# THE HEAT OF ACTION

ALL IS QUIET AROUND THE HOUSE WHERE ARIBERT HEIM IS STAYING. IT IS PAST MIDNIGHT. We have left our vehicles several hundred yards away. John and Roger go off to one side, Paul and I to the other. We are equipped with infra-red glasses, thermal suits and heavy, waterproof shoes. We move forward as silently as possible in the snow, Paul and I each carrying on our backs a quiver stuffed full of metal arrows and a sophisticated bow. Silently, we make towards the principal residence. After a dozen yards, we veer off towards the enormous wooden shed that serves as barn, storehouse and wood store. The building protects the house from prying eyes.

We stop fifty yards from the shed and light the torch that we have stuck in the snow. Followed by Paul, I seize my bow and position an arrow, the tip of which is wrapped in a cloth soaked in inflammable liquid. In less than a minute, we have all shot four arrows each towards the rear part of the shed. Two of mine penetrate inside, piercing a bit of cardboard that is covering the side window; the two others reach the wooden wall, which begins to go up in flames. More battle-experienced than I in handling a bow, Paul manages to send his four arrows inside the structure, by aiming for a fanlight near the ceiling. They land in some haystacks. In a single moment, the shed lights up, transforming into a giant torch. The fire takes hold and has soon consumed the contents of the shed. Surprised by the violence of the fire, we withdraw before beating a retreat and disappearing into the night.

Our companions responsible for electronic surveillance capture shouts and screaming in German. In the house is the pandemonium of combat. The fire is advancing and thick, black smoke pours from it, accompanied by the strong smell of burning rubber. A little group rushes outside, one of the men brandishing a rifle with a telescopic sight. At the very moment that Aribert Heim's front wave of men arrives outside the shed, the house is suddenly plunged into darkness. John and Roger have just sabotaged a transformer, causing a massive short-circuit. In the house, the shouts redouble. Other men come out with buckets of water and they are soon all fighting the fire with the energy of despair. Huddled into the darkness, several dozen yards away, we savour the spectacle. The damage was only material. More's the pity…

Several minutes later, all that is left of the shed is a few burning remains, which the resigned Nazis no longer even try to put out. Hcim's men are overwhelmed by the violence and speed with which the flames have devoured their prey. They have not called the fire service and no one has come to their rescue. The residence is isolated, far from the houses of the town; the fire was started late at night and it is even possible that no one has seen anything.

Shortly afterwards, our mikes capture the conversations between the Nazis. They are furious — and worried. The concomitance of the fire and the power cut has not escaped them. Some advance the possibility of sabotage, an attack. They decide to redouble their caution. As for us, our mission is accomplished: the fire has flushed out the rats, allowing us to update our list. There are more than we thought. It is our turn to be worried...

*

Day breaks to a scene of desolation. The wind has plastered the outside of the house with soot. Opposite, a few dozen yards away, all that remains of the shed is an enormous pile of charred wood and metal carcasses. Despite the biting cold, we feel warm inside. We scrutinise the terrain through our binoculars. I remain immobile and focus on a clump of bushes 800 yards from the house. Paul has done the same.

'What is that?'

'It looks like smoke…'

If we draw a straight line between the shed and the smoking bush, we are not far from the place where we filmed Herbert on his bike the first time. We have finally found the tunnel! It is linked directly to the shed and doubtless also to Elsa and Berti's house. The bushes, doubtless planted there deliberately, hide the air holes.

The team members we have left on lookout at the site with a radio see Elsa and Berti wandering around the ruins of the barn and sifting through the debris. Rolf, Marcus's son, joins them, followed by another, older man — this is Gunther, Roda's husband. (We had thought that these two Nazis, high up on the list of friends likely to give refuge to Heim in case of problems, were hiding away on Kodiak Island in Alaska.) The little group wanders around, helpless and incredulous, amid the still smoking ashes. We wonder what on earth they can be looking for…

In the afternoon, our lookout group notice that all the windows on the ground floor are wide open, to allow fresh air in and to get rid of the remains of the smoke; its acrid smell, doubtless unbearable, fills the house and continues to emerge from the air holes of the tunnel — impossible to go in there without an oxygen mask and protective gear. All its entrances and those of the house would have to be left open for several days to clear the atmosphere inside; this is obviously incompatible with the security measures adopted by Aribert Heim's bodyguards.

The tunnel remains closed over the following days. Why do Heim's friends who are inside the house not risk airing it, despite the danger of toxic gases? They are suspicious. Doubtless they have realised that the noose is tightening around them, that the fire was arson and that their electric transformer was sabotaged. Knowing they are being watched, they prefer not to run any risk. Do they know we have discovered the tunnel? In any event, they do not know that we have seized the advantage.

Our electronic tapping of the house gives us confirmation that its occupants have no intention of using the tunnel or even of checking its state. On our side, we are determined to take advantage of the situation. Barney asks the logistical branch of the organisation to procure insulating suits and respiratory apparatus like that used in disaster site rescue operations for us, so that we can work securely in what is likely to be extremely polluted conditions. After nightfall, Paul and I put on our thick suits again, activate our nocturnal vision glasses and take our respiratory equipment to launch an attack on the smoking bush. We have no trouble locating the little shaft covered with a metal grille. We undo the base, making as little noise as possible, and keeping an eye on the house and surroundings. After working for an hour and a half, we have pierced a hole big enough to allow us to enter the tunnel.

The tenacious odour of the smoke confirms our hypothesis: the tunnel is swimming in ash dust. We open our oxygen bottles and put on our airproof masks. A last check of our protective equipment and we slip into the tunnel interior. We move forward with great caution. Because of the darkness we have to use pocket torches; the passageway is about two yards high and its width allows a man of normal size to move. On the ground, rudimentary rails seem to have been placed to allow the passage of a small wagon. On the side runs a cable that must take electric current from the shed. We mark our entrance point with an infra-red light and make our way away from the house, slowly, like two astronauts on the moon, examining the walls with meticulous attention.

Not far from the entrance, we come across the snowbike and the trailer that we saw full of equipment and provisions. The tunnel has been enlarged at this spot and, beside the trailer, we discover a small wagon, like those used in mines; it must serve to transport things directly to the shed. Paul gets a plastic envelope containing locksmith's material out of his suit. He takes a print of the lock on the massive, crude padlock that closes the inside of the entrance door to the tunnel and prepares a mould of the key, while I lean on the motorbike — out of action.

Once Paul has finished his work, we turn around and make our way towards the other end of the tunnel. We long to know if it stops at the house or at the ruins of the shed. A little worried, we nonetheless decide to check out the site from the other side. Our suits are covered with black and brown soot stains. An unbelievable amount of ash has accumulated in the tunnel; the ground and the metal rails are totally covered in it, in a thick, crumbly layer. Every time we take a step, we make a crater and raise a cloud of blinding brown dust. We slow down, attentive to our slightest movements, taking calculated precautions for fear of knocking into some object that could be buried under this sea of soot.

Finally, we reach a large metal door. Twisted by the heat of the fire, it seems to be suspended in the void, threatening to collapse at any moment. Though we want to continue our inspection of the place, we satisfy ourselves with a quick glance through the burnt and deformed doorway, towards what looks in the darkness like a courtyard in which everything has been consumed and destroyed. On the other side, the tunnel ends under the shed. We examine the walls in the hope of finding a hidden door – in vain. We are forced to the unfortunate conclusion that if there is a tunnel linking the house to the shed, it is not this one.

Before leaving, we hide two electronic alarm devices under a little heap of ash, alongside the rails. All contact with the mechanism, however light, will send signals to the surveillance post at which we all take turns of duty: we will thus be immediately informed about the smallest movement in the tunnel.

The return journey is slow and difficult. After a long while, I catch sight of the infra-red light that marks the air hole by which we came in. I let loose a sigh of relief and turn towards Paul:

'You look like a mole... Except that moles stink less than you do!'

I burst out laughing and receive in reply a punch on the shoulder that lifts a huge mushroom of dust and black soot. My mask has slipped and the soot chokes me. I get out of the tunnel as fast as I can, leaving behind me a laughing Paul. His rapid movements and the brusque jump that he executes coming out of the air hole only dislodge yet more dust into the tunnel. Fresh air! At last!

A little later, back at Orleans Island, Paul tells our friends, assembled to hear our report in the meeting room of our HQ:

'We have just been to a fireman's surprise party and it was extraordinary; next time, we'll invite you.'

Bowled over by the description of the damage caused by the fire, they question us about the possibility of an access tunnel to the Nazis' house.

'It doesn't make sense,' exclaims John, 'there must be a tunnel that goes right up to the house. I'm sure of it!'

We assure him that it's impossible but John refuses to accept it and insists on visiting the tunnel himself with Paul, that very evening.

\*

We have a fine day, finally giving us the opportunity to recommence our aerial reconnaissance. Given the rapid changes of climate in the region, we have to take advantage of the mild weather. Paul and John carry out the technical preparations that will allow them to get into the tunnel, after nightfall. Barney,

# THE HEAT OF ACTION

Roger, Gerald and I get ourselves ready for a session of aerial photography above the town of Tadoussac and along the big fjord up to the town of Chicoutimi and around Lake St John. Our objective: to gather as many details as possible about the refuges likely to harbour Aribert Heim and his accomplices. The rest of the team is deployed around the house.

An hour later, the helicopter soars above Orleans Island. The planned flight is quite complicated and the various tasks are divided up to ensure maximum efficiency. Gerald is responsible for photography, I am in charge of the helicopter for the first part of the trip and Roger will take care of the return journey – he needs a certain number of flight hours for his pilot's licence. Seated behind, next to Gerald, Barney studies the maps and the photos of the various sites we will be flying over. The helicopter turns towards the south and, thirty seconds later, we are above the St Lawrence, heading north north-east towards St Joachim.

'Go ahead, start the camera and the video,' Barney says to Gerald, who is snapping the access routes between St Joachim and Cape Torment and the river.

Barney is convinced that Aribert Heim will choose one of these routes if he escapes to the sea – although the information we have gathered points to the contrary. He sweeps aside our arguments, declaring that Heim and his friends have mounted a disinformation campaign to deceive listening ears.

We cross over the place twice without getting too close to St Joachim, before making for the east, at 800 metres altitude, along the line of the coast. From time to time, Gerald films the places that could serve as shelter. I slalom between the small clouds at low altitude and, in order to have better visibility, dive down 400 hundred yards towards the woods, the mountains and the snow-covered towns. The helicopter flies over the frozen water courses and along the St Lawrence, sitting imperturbably in the middle of this picture postcard landscape. We go around the marvellous little town of St Paul and its bay, at the entrance to the Gouffre river. On our right, the Coudres islands and its frozen estuary.

Barney and Roger, seated behind, remain silent throughout almost the whole of the flight. Barney is immersed in a little album of photos and Roger has his nose pressed up against the helicopter porthole, studying the landscape attentively as if trying to find something he has lost in the snowy fields. From time to time, he scribbles notes in a little book.

In the distance, on the northern bank of the St Lawrence, the green roofs of Manoir Richelieu stand out against a white background. The bank of the river, loaded with snow, slopes down fairly steeply towards water that contains large blocks of ice, all jostling against each other close to the bank. It is not an ideal spot in which to take refuge. The helicopter then makes its way towards the little town of St Simeon. We fly over the junction of Route 170 towards the west, in the direction of Chicoutimi on the south side of Saguenay fjord. Holding our breath, we skim the top of the old lighthouse on Dog's Head Cape and its gulf.

We have got to the fjord and can see the town of Tadoussac on the eastern bank. Built on several hillsides, its southern side gives onto a little creek with a modest port. We fly over this picturesque, peaceful little town, then continue eastwards as planned. I begin a large circle over the river and head for the town, right to the port. Gerald takes the opportunity to exercise his talents as photographer. Several seconds before we fly over the tongue of land that separates the port from the edge of the fjord, he signals to me to veer to the left, towards the south of the fjord. There, it is impossible to get away via the river unless one has use of an icebreaker, which is doubtless not the case in Aribert Heim's organisation. To the west is a gigantic, completely deserted stretch of ice; the surrounding sides are covered in untouched snow, the trees in the woods labouring under their white burden. In the middle of this arctic landscape runs Route 170, the vital axis of communication, cleared regularly by snowploughs. We continue on to Chicoutimi, moving south-west.

Roger communicates our next objective to me: a cottage situated north of the Peribonka river, on the edge of forest and frozen lake country. It is an extraordinary and bleak region in which the temperature, both day and night, is measured in tens of degrees below zero. The helicopter flies over the town of Alma, then, after several miles above the water line of Lake St John, it veers towards the north and flies over the twists and turns of the Peribonka river. This is where Elsa and Berti's summer lodge, their favourite holiday resort, is located. We can see it clearly: built on two storeys, in the middle of trees, it is perfectly integrated into the landscape – totally isolated, planted at the end of the world, in a desert of virtually inaccessible ice. Judging by the amount of snow surrounding it, it has not been visited for a long time. Perfect. This isolation will allow us to use the whole range of special operational methods at our disposal, without fear of killjoys.

A doubt gnaws at me. All this seems too good to be true. What if Aribert Heim and his men are leading us by the nose? I am prepared to bet that our prey will not come to the chalet except as a last resort.

Just under a mile from our target, I land the helicopter right in the middle of the frozen river. Roger and Gerald move off, treading carefully over the icy, slippery ground, waddling like a couple of penguins. They return a few minutes later:

'Hell, this wretched ice is thick!' says Roger. 'I've never seen anything like it. It's at least fifteen inches.'

A small step for the penguins, a huge step for The Owl...

# CHAPTER 12
# THE MORT

I N ST JOACHIM, AROUND THE NAZI RESIDENCE, THE FROZEN HOURS FOLLOW ON ONE AFTER THE OTHER, ALL IDENTICAL. Our sentries still have nothing to report; no one comes in or goes out of the house and the electronic listening devices record no significant conversation. The beast has gone to ground and is waiting. Barney, Roger and I take advantage of the lull to go down to New York to get exchange parts for our electronic installations, our listening system and our helicopter.

My friend Giora comes to get us in a little private plane, a 'Cherokee', hired at Long Island airport. Barney leaves us as the plane starts its descent. It is best that he is not there for the ensuing events; useless to expose him more than necessary. We all pile into a monospace and set off for a smart area of the city, near the airport.

Giora is a precious element because of his contacts. We have given him a mission of trust: to find a supplier for our equipment. He takes us to one of his friends, who welcomes us with a large smile to his luxurious residence. After a warm exchange of handshakes, he takes us to his cellar where the material we have requested is piled up. Even if the aeronautical club to which Giora's friend belongs is perfectly respectable, certain of his other activities are less so. With a half-smile, he offers to sell us other 'exchange parts' and leads us into his 'showroom' where we find, carefully set out on a games table, dozens of firearms — pistols, personal missiles, grenades, bazookas, heavy machine guns... Enough to equip a small army.

'If an exchange part interests you, don't hesitate to make an order. I am unbeatable on price and delivery times. All my products are at the cutting edge of technology. You won't find them anywhere else on the market.'

Giora's friend does not realise that we already have in our possession several of his 'exclusive' products! Roger gives a polite refusal and we load our boxes into the van.

Giora drives at great speed through the streets of this calm district and gets back on the motorway, heading for Queens, where Barney is waiting for us in his luxurious home; he directs us into the rear courtyard. We place the material in one of the rooms, which Barney locks. Giora takes me to one side to ask me news about his friend in Montreal.

'He's perfect... I don't know what we would have done without him.'

'He is entirely trustworthy. He is an unconditional supporter of Israel.'

I smile to myself. Giora is still convinced that he is working for Mossad... Useless to set him straight.

'What about Jo?'

'We've reached a stalemate.'

'What happened? I don't understand, I was expecting to receive a wedding invitation!'

Difficult to say. Perhaps she has got scared by the speed with which our relationship began. She is supposed to arrive in New York for the weekend and we have left it that she will tell me what time she is to land so that I can go and get her. But I've had no news... Perhaps she has cancelled her trip? On the phone several hours later, Jo doesn't dare tell me that she is indeed not coming. End of the affair. Perhaps I should have talked to her about The Owl, Aribert Heim and what I am really doing?

No time to feel sorry for myself. An important meeting awaits us. We have to prepare for our return to Canada, planned for the following day. Once again, our group splits up: I form a team with Roger, while Barney stays behind to take care of his numerous affairs, somewhat neglected as a result of our Canadian activities... We discuss the methods of getting through the border and of transporting special equipment.

Around nine o'clock in the evening, Barney leaves us for a

business meeting and we continue to fine-tune the details of the operation. It is essential that we finalise arrangements with Giora. His role is now much more important than it has been and he is taking many more risks. Towards midnight, Roger withdraws into his room while I take the opportunity to have an open and frank conversation with Giora. I try to dissuade him from getting too involved – we can do without him... But he is determined to take part:

'I will go with you to the very end!' he says. 'It's past the point of no return now.'

\*

The cold wind blowing over Long Island airport bites into our faces and takes our breath away. We jump up and down and stamp our feet in front of the twin-engined Chieftain hired by Giora, while we wait for the technical preparations to be completed. A flight to the north-east of the United States in the middle of winter is no small undertaking, even in a plane known to be safe and reliable; the tiniest lack of attention could have tragic consequences. Several minutes later, the Chieftain's engines are throbbing and the regulators working at full power. The plane starts its run on the wet airfield, devouring the distance to the take-off point. Once the engine is at full stretch, Giora pulls the control lever towards him and the plane rises in a single movement.

The weather improves and, apart from several small air

pockets, nothing spoils the pleasure of the flight. Even the stopover at Brewer, a little airport near the town of Bangor in Maine, doesn't affect our good humour. The last reconnaissance point on our route, St Froid Lake indicates that we have almost reached our goal. We fly over a basic, isolated runway; the plane veers to the right and makes for the waymark of red smoke that John has placed at the start of the icy track. Touching down, the plan skids alarmingly. Demonstrating exemplary cool, Giora masters the situation without too much difficulty. The apparatus comes to a stop and the beating of our hearts calms...

Gerald and John, who have come to greet us – and who were terrified by our acrobatic landing – take things in hand:

'We have a lot on our plate and very little time to eat it! We have to get the equipment off the plane quickly.'

We transfer weapons, luggage and boxes of electronic material to a caravan hired by John and Gerald. Officially, it serves as an ornithological research laboratory – in reality, it is our moving weapons store. A recognised NGO, the 'International Ornithology Association' enjoys all the necessary authorisations. We can come and go without problems, on both sides of the American-Canadian border.

Not without a slight pull at the heart, I watch Giora leave. John and Gerald make a hasty departure on their four-wheel drive, which is towing the enormous caravan; Roger and I follow them half an hour later in the old vehicle that Gerald bought for barely 300 dollars. Leaving a gap of half an hour means that we won't all arrive at the border at the same time...

When we arrived at the border post, a young policeman gives us a cheerful greeting and asks to see our passports. He looks with curiosity at the insignias we are sporting on the back of our shirts and Roger hurriedly explains:

'They are the logos of the International Ornithology Association; we are doing research into endangered bird species.'

Roger is convincing. He gives a little ornithology leaflet to the border guard and, several minutes later, we are on the other side of the frontier, in the district of New Brunswick, driving to meet John and Gerald. We are returning to the house – the hunt is back on.

In our old bone shaker, we take the little road that winds its way through a huge, snow-covered forest. The car slips, slides, jumps and dances the whole of the white route. Not far from the place where we are to meet John, Roger stops the car. I get out of the vehicle and take off the number plates. Roger steers the car straight into the trunk of one of the enormous trees all around us. The collision provokes a fall of snow that almost entirely covers the vehicle. Roger drags himself on his stomach from the car, which we finish concealing before going back onto the little road. After more than a mile of energetic walking in the snow, we rediscover our companions, who are waiting for us in the warmth of the caravan.

'Orleans, here we come!'

*

Three hours later, we arrive on Orleans Island, where Jane, Suzanne and Sharon are waiting for us. When we see Harry, who should have been out on the ground, we realise that something is going on.

'There is some interesting news,' he says to us, his voice full of enthusiasm. 'They are all on action stations in Aribert Heim's hideout. The conspiracy of silence is over!'

'It's high time,' murmurs John.

'Heim has lost consciousness, his health has deteriorated,' recounts Jane, who was the first to decipher the recordings in German. 'Elsa contacted one of her friends for him to be admitted urgently to a hospital in Quebec province. She was panicky on the telephone; she had asked her friend to do everything in his power to allow the hospitalisation to take place in the greatest discretion and for their "guest" to be kept in the most total isolation...'

We are hanging on to Jane's every word. She interrupts her account to catch her breath, looks at us, gathers herself, then concludes:

'Half an hour later, the friend in question rang Elsa back to announce that everything had been arranged. He added, before hanging up: "Give me two hours warning before you arrive and we'll look after everything."'

That same evening, John and Gerald reinforce the surveillance team. 10 pm: our lookout people signal abnormal activity in the house and around the garage. The occupants are preparing to break camp. We immediately swing into action.

Followed by Roger, I make straight for the helicopter. We need several hours to put all the material brought from New York on board.

Lit by a torch, we work in a temperature of minus 10. From time to time, Suzanne brings us boiling-hot coffee and informs us of the latest news. The light of the garage in Aribert Heim's house has been on for many hours. Thanks to the electronic equipment at their disposal, our lookout team is following the preparations for the departure of Heim's friends. The door of the main building remains closed. However, inside is incessant activity: the Nazis must be using an underground passage that links the house to the garage, more than thirty yards away.

While we check the functioning of the various systems we have just installed on the helicopter, Sharon comes running up:

'John wants to speak to one of you immediately.'

Roger speeds over to the house. A quarter of an hour later he is back:

'Thank God, the action is beginning!' he declares with elation. 'The Nazis are leaving tomorrow. They are escaping! Our mates on the ground have intercepted all their conversations. Their situation is disastrous and their nerves are on edge. Heim's health seems to be worsening and they are in a great hurry...'

The Nazis are going to split up. Karl and Monika are leaving to take refuge in Germany. Herbert has decided to disappear into the forests of north Canada, and will hide in the chalet near the Peribonka river that we have already identified during our previous missions. Rolf, with whom he served in the SS, will doubtless join him. Gunther, Roda, Dino and Sophie have decided to take a flight back home. It is Elsa and Berti who will take care of Heim and escort him to the hospital, joined by the three friends who have been helping them until now.

As head of the operation, John communicates instructions to each of the members. We are organised into small action groups: from their surveillance post, Paul and Sean have a very good view of the house and the terrain. It is they who will give the green light to all the commandos waiting at their post. John and Sharon (platoon number one) and Harry and Suzanne (platoon number two) will watch the two exits from St Joachim towards the east and the west, by the only main road, Route 138. Roger and me (platoon number three) are responsible for aerial surveillance. We also have to assist the others in case of need. Gerald and Jane (platoon number four) are for their part charged with the surveillance of Aribert Heim. We are counting on Jane's reputation in the medical world to obtain the most recent, confidential details on the rat's state of health, once we have located the hospital.

Barney, who was supposed to stay in New York several days longer for his business affairs, comes back earlier than planned and co-ordinates operations from the building on Orleans Island. He is to be our campaign leader.

\*

Very early in the morning, the tapping devices reveal that the situation inside the hideout is rapidly deteriorating. The Nazis decide to bring forward the hospitalisation of our prey. Around eight o'clock, Paul communicates the arrival of an ambulance. The lady driver makes her way slowly towards Elsa and Berti's house. She looks for the road, hesitates, then accelerates and heads for the door of the house whereupon Elsa, who has been watching the arrival of the vehicle from a window, goes out to meet the new arrivals. A tall man in his sixties, with white hair, gets out of the ambulance; he is wearing a doctor's coat and carrying a briefcase in his hand. The driver, a woman in her thirties, joins him in the courtyard. She is carrying a stretcher and a first-aid kit – doubtless a nurse. Elsa salutes them with her hand, giving no other form of acknowledgement, and takes them inside.

'She seems tense and impatient,' Paul says to us over the radio.

'Let's hope the bastard isn't dying!' declares Roger. 'I hope he suffers as he has never suffered…'

Two hours later, the driver of the ambulance comes out of the house and takes the vehicle to the rear courtyard.

'Things are moving, the rat is on the point of departure…' Sean alerts us from his post behind the house.

'They've opened the rear door of the ambulance. Here it is. He's coming out!'

Thanks to our electronic equipment, Sean, despite the distance between him and the house, has a ringside seat. Two men are carrying Aribert Heim on a stretcher. Once in the ambulance, the nurse and the doctor connect him up to a drip and put an oxygen mask on him.

The Nazis' escape has been very well organised. While Elsa and the medical team have been making themselves busy around the rat, the rest of the band must have been using this famous underground tunnel, which we have not located, to leave the house, for the garage doors open suddenly and, at the very moment that the ambulance leaves the property, the three cars that were parked in the garage come hurtling out.

Berti is driving the first; on board are Gunther, Roda, Dino and Sophie. In the second vehicle is the most dangerous element of the group: Rolf, the irascible brute, who is at the steering wheel; at his side, another Nazi war criminal on the run, Herbert. He seems as tense as a coiled-up spring and constantly looks around in all directions. So it is these two who are to go to the chalet on the bank of the Peribonka river, in northern Canada. The third car is driven by Karl, his wife Monika sitting beside him. Behind, we make out three people but can identify only two – the individuals who had got Aribert Heim into Canada. The four vehicles, the ambulance at the head, leave the property at full speed, then the cortege divides. Herbert and Rolf take the north-east direction and are absorbed into Route 138, which joins the motorway.

'The birds are taking flight.'

Seated in the helicopter, ready to intervene since dawn,

Roger and I jump when we hear the agreed signal on the radio. Less than five minutes later, we are in the air and speeding towards the theatre of operations. We fly over the ambulance making towards the town of Quebec. Berti's car takes the direction of the airport, followed at a distance by Harry and Suzanne's vehicle. Thanks to our tapping devices, we know that Dino, Gunther and their wives have booked flights to Anchorage in Alaska, from where they will leave for their final destination, Kodiak Island. Harry and Suzanne have reserved two seats on the same flight.

At Barney's request, we lend a hand to Paul and Sean, who are following Karl, Monika and their three acolytes. We quickly identify the Nazis' car. It is already in St Joachim and is making straight for the church, where it stops, right outside the building. Monika gets out and runs into it. Shortly afterwards, Paul also makes his way into the church. He sees Monika praying, crossing herself then moving towards the organ. She busies herself around the instrument before leaving again. Paul waits until she has disappeared before inspecting the old organ, behind which he discovers a hiding place in which an envelope has been placed. He stuffs it into the inner pocket of his coat and, several seconds later, he is outside.

Meanwhile, on board the helicopter, we are flying over the woods around while awaiting new instructions. They are not long in coming. Sean takes the microphone:

'Owl Four to Owl One, the car is leaving the church.'

'Understood, Owl Four, we'll start tailing them again.'

# THE MORT

We turn the helicopter towards St Joachim and have no trouble spotting the Nazis' vehicle. Sean has given a report of what has happened to Barney, who responds:

'Owl Four, this is Mum. Wait near the church...'

After a few minutes, Paul and Sean glimpse a small car coming from the other end of the street which parks in front of the church. A fairly elderly blonde woman is at the steering wheel. She waits a while, studies the street and the sculpture-filled park opposite, then gets out and goes into the church. Sean, who has been filming her since her arrival, can now see her in the telescopic lens; while she is coming out of the church, he notices her confused, perturbed expression, as if she has just witnessed some disaster. She hurriedly gets back into her car and turns around without waiting. Paul and Sean tail her until she gets back home, Sean taking photos of the car and the house – we will check who owns it later. Paul and Sean then get back onto Route 138. We direct them to Karl and Monika's car.

'Hurry up!' I say to them. 'They're coming into the suburbs of Quebec, you're going to lose them!'

Several moments later, Paul has re-established visual contact with his prey. We leave them to return to our new target, Herbert and Rolf. Roger soon identifies John and Sharon's car and, in front, a short distance away, that of the two Nazis. Rolf and Herbert are careful not to be noticed, scrupulously respecting the highway code; nothing in their behaviour betrays that they are preoccupied or that they suspect they are being followed. They seem more like innocent tourists than criminals anxious to save their skin. Several times I move off to the right or the left before rejoining my flight path, so as not to be spotted myself. The Nazis approach the town of St Simeon, from where the route to Lake St John begins.

'They are doubtless going to take the 170...' John says to me over the radio. 'I suggest we go ahead of them, cutting directly to Saguenay fjord.'

'Okay, affirmative. Go on. I'll stay for a bit to see what they're doing.'

John goes ahead of the Nazis and gets onto Route 170. But there is a change of direction at the last moment and they continue on the 180.

'Turn around! They're not going to Lake St John, they are continuing on the 180.'

'We're retracing our steps! Don't lose sight of them. We must stop them escaping at all costs. At all costs!'

John and Sharon launch into pursuit of Herbert and Rolf.

'Hurry up,' says Roger to John. 'The car has got to the south bank of Saguenay fjord. It's in the queue waiting to go up onto the ferry to Tadoussac. It's the last one, loading in several minutes. You're going to miss them, get a move on!'

The cars go up onto the ferry and the siren sounds. Too late for John and Sharon. They will get the next ferry. A sailor casts off and the vessel moves into the distance; my friends' car has still not arrived.

After having informed Barney of the new developments, we

draw up a plan B. Once the ferry has anchored on the other side of the fjord, the Nazis' car leaves the jetty and heads towards the Tadoussac house. On the opposite side of the river, John and Sharon's car drives onto the following ferry. The distance between the two cars, between the hunter and its prey, is widening. Above all, we must not lose sight of the Nazis, until John and Sharon catch them up.

Herbert and Rolf's car drives up the main street, turns into a small road at the foot of the hill and takes the direction of the port before moving onto another pathway bordering the fjord's estuary. It slows down in front of an elegant chalet and enters its small courtyard. From a distance, I see the two men getting out of the car. One of them is carrying a large sports bag. The door opens, an elderly individual comes out, shakes their hands and asks them inside.

Twenty minutes later, guided by Roger on the radio, John and Sharon arrive at the corner of the small street running alongside the creek and park their car in a spot where they have a full view of the house in which the Nazis have taken refuge. The arrival of our comrades means we can move off. We feared that the noise of the engine would awaken the suspicions of our target or the police, even if we have been careful to fly high enough not to be heard.

We land the helicopter on a little tourist airport on the outskirts of St Simeon. As soon as he is told of our function as members of the International Ornithology Association, the manager of the aeroclub gives us a VIP welcome. Our research into threatened bird species enjoys great success and expressions of support flood in, as do offers of help and service, as well as ideas for our research work... We take advantage of all of this to gather more precise information about the area, concentrating particularly on aeronautical clubs in the region. This is how we learn that one of the private air companies, located beside a frozen lake seven miles north of Tadoussac, carries out flights to distant destinations. This company owns a plane that can land in snow. It carries passengers and material to the bleak, frozen wastelands in the north of Canada. This plane could easily deposit our two Nazis on the frozen Peribonka river, near the chalet, thereby allowing them to disappear, unknown to everybody. That seems to us the most plausible hypothesis. We decide to explore this trail, in the hope of getting ahead of our prey.

The plane in question, we are told, has undertaken only one flight early that morning, before returning to the north, to Forestville airport where it is to undergo a technical check. If the Nazis want to use this company's services to escape, they cannot do so before tomorrow morning.

We immediately telephone the company's office to ask about the possibility of making a flight to the town of Alma, on the edge of Lake St John, the following day.

'I'm really sorry,' replies the assistant, who has a strong Quebecker accent, 'tomorrow there are no more places on the plane...'

'But there is a flight to Alma?' asks Roger.

'It's a private flight… I am not allowed to tell you where it's going.'

'At least tell me what time it's leaving.'

'I can't.'

'Be nice… I work for the International Ornithology Association. I have to send two cages of rare birds that are invaluable for the research work of a colleague at Lavalle University as soon as possible. She's in the Lake St John region and she's waiting for them impatiently. Do you think the plane could make a stopover to deliver the cages?'

'Okay, listen… Keep it to yourself but the plane has to go north of Alma… It has a very tight schedule and there is no possibility of making a stopover because there are other commitments. It is supposed to take passengers and equipment, then return immediately.'

*

Standing next to the helicopter, we decide on a change of organisation: Paul will join us while Sean, for his part, leaves the little airport and takes Route 170 which borders the fjord. The helicopter, stuffed with equipment, takes off several minutes later in a westerly direction. The terrain is clear but covered with snow; I have no idea what is waiting for us. I hesitate to land:

'If the ground isn't stable, the helicopter could react badly and I don't intend to make an emergency stop.'

After a risky manoeuvre, I finally manage to land, just long enough for Paul and Roger to unload the material; they check they haven't forgotten anything and signal to me. I immediately take off again, while they leave to explore the banks of the Peribonka river. All along the 170, I pass overhead Sean's car:

'Owl Three, this is Owl One. Our friends are waiting for us. It is freezing cold and the routes are snow-bound. Be careful, where you're going, the snowploughs haven't ventured.'

Not far from St Simeon, I establish contact with John and Sharon, who are still watching the house in which Herbert and Rolf have taken refuge, observing the two men's hideout through binoculars and listening to their conversations. In the evening, they make do with the satellite microphone to spy on the house. From his observation post, Sharon makes out the filtered light coming through the badly drawn curtains upstairs. The rest of the house is plunged in darkness.

\*

A kind of paradise on earth in my eyes, Orleans Island is my house. The building in which we have set up our headquarters symbolises incomparable friendship, loyalty and openness. However, this time, it is with no pleasure that I land on our improvised heliport. The place is deserted; all my comrades are on the ground. Overwhelmed by the silence reigning in the house, I remember the familiar, joyous hubbub of our past meetings, our enthusiastic discussions and Paul and Roger's altercations; I would give a lot to be able to hear Suzanne and experience her robust embrace, or to see Sharon's angelic face. But the person I miss most is John, that extraordinary, noisy and extravagant man who is the heart of our organisation. I find it hard to accept that all my friends are outside, in conditions that are far from pleasant, while I am preparing to spend nights between sheets, well sheltered from harsh weather conditions. It doesn't take me long to prepare the material that I have to transport the following day. I cannot calm myself down and spend the evening wandering around the house, and the night tossing and turning in my bed, prey to one of the worst bouts of insomnia of my life. Around four o'clock in the morning, I drop off for barely half an hour before the alarm clock goes off.

The piping hot coffee puts my thoughts in order. I go out onto the terrace to get a little fresh air; all my senses violently awakened by the icy morning air, I feel ready to face a new day. I will make up for my lack of sleep later... The darkness is replaced by the breaking light of day.

I make for the helicopter, finish the flight preparations and take off once more, flying over the St Lawrence at low altitude. Once in the middle of the river, I gain altitude, flying along the river's edge, and then turn in a north-easterly direction heading for St Simeon airport. Several moments before landing, I make contact with John:

'I'm about to arrive. As we agreed, I'll land and wait on standby...'

Several minutes later, a little before nine o'clock in the morning, I am beginning my descent towards the airport when John's low, precise voice resonates in the receiver:

'Be careful. There are movements in the house; I have the feeling our friends are not going to be long. Be ready to move in.'

At half-past nine, when the two Nazis make their appearance in the courtyard, the helicopter is already in the air. I see Rolf coming out first. On the alert, he looks around with great caution. He is carrying a large bag slung over his shoulder – doubtless weapons, their 'insurance policies', which they will not hesitate to use. Two minutes later, a taxi stops in front of the house. Herbert joins Rolf outside, a road map in his hand. The taxi driver puts his skiing equipment in the boot while they take leave of the house's owner. John follows the three men's conversation: the owner is reluctant to have the car left in front of the house, even when they promise that a friend will come to get it in a few hours. A small sum of money succeeds in quashing his reservations. The taxi sets off east, taking the main highway in Tadoussac, Route 138; the helicopter is already flying over the site of the little air company. At the extremity of the magnificent lake, very close by, I make out the wooden jetty at the end of which is a water plane. John and Sharon are following the two Nazis from afar and are careful to keep their distance.

'As planned, they are making for the lake,' John tells me over the radio.

## THE MORT

The taxi stops in front of the air company's office. John and Sharon have been following its route by the lake and, along the way, have seen the taxi driver get two huge bags out of the boot. John accelerates, and then stops after several miles, on a promontory from where they can watch the lake. Two minutes later, John's voice rings out over the radio:

'Things are happening!'

There is a powerful throbbing and the water plane rises up above the lake before moving away. I land the helicopter and John climbs aboard. Sharon has already taken the route for Orleans Island once more when we launch into pursuit of the water plane. It is flying far ahead of us, several hundred feet above our helicopter's line of altitude. John studies the map of the region and comments that the plane is making for one of the chalets photographed during our reconnaissance flights, dozens of miles from the chalet that we had thought would serve as refuge to the Nazis. We have to change plan. I immediately inform our teams and communicate our new bearings to them. With their snowbikes, Roger's team can be on the spot in twenty minutes or so. If they hurry, it's workable.

I begin a rapid descent towards the tops of the trees after identifying a landing place, far from the plane's view, near a clump of trees from which we have unobstructed sight of the Nazis' new retreat. I land the helicopter and cut off the motor. We hear the engine noise of the approaching water plane — several moments later, it lands on the lake.

211

We are waiting in the enveloping silence of the Great North. Soon, we hear the throbbing of the plane engine again, taking off and moving away into the distance. From where we are, we catch sight of the two Nazis, loaded down with equipment, advancing towards the second chalet, five or six miles from the spot where Roger and Paul are waiting for them. I contact my two friends on the radio.

'The rats have changed route. They're no longer coming towards you. They are going towards chalet number 3. If you hurry, you could arrive before them.'

I am mad with rage.

Pity that the helicopter is not armed; I would willingly have released one or two rockets...

'It all seems very strange to me,' says John. 'They seem even better organised than we imagined.'

'I don't know. Perhaps the three chalets belong to the Nazi gang? But if so, why haven't we known about it?'

'I know just how furious Roger is going to be. He hates our plans being wrongfooted.'

The Nazis disappear into the rear yard of the chalet. We do not have to wait long. After an hour, the sound of an engine reverberates and two brand new snowbikes spring up from the snowy bank, slipping onto the frozen surface of the river. The two men's backpacks are full and they each have a rifle at their side. John and I are already in the helicopter. We have only to warm up the engine and then we are in the sky, from where we have no difficulty spotting the two Nazis. They stop half a mile or so from their hideout to study their map and discuss something, before moving off again. Herbert in front and Rolf following him. They have not spotted us: I am flying at too high an altitude. Soon, we can no longer make them out with the naked eye; I descend and fly over the treetops on the opposite bank. John switches on the camera and turns it towards the two snowbikes. He studies the length and breadth of the river, lingering over the snow-covered banks, and then comes back to the surface of the river, which is completely frozen over.

The Nazis slow down from time to time, hampered by the obstacles of snow and ice, which they pass without too much difficulty. Just over a mile from the chalet, they suddenly stop and inspect the surrounding terrain, as if they suspected an ambush. A brief confab ensues, accompanied by vehement gestures. Herbert takes off his backpack, takes hold of his rifle and places it on the passenger seat. He starts his snowbike up again and departs, leaving his friend Rolf behind him.

At the end of the pathway leading off from the river, several dozen metres from the second chalet, the Nazi parks his vehicle and gets off. He inspects the chalet and its surroundings and moves slowly, apparently full of apprehension, towards the rear yard which is entirely covered in virgin snow. Danger will not come from this side: the snow is too deep.

Herbert retraces his steps, moving along the outside wall of the chalet to check the shutters on the ground floor.

Suddenly, the first floor shutters open with a click: it's Roger, who was waiting to make an ambush in the chalet. Paul is not far away, covering him. The two men had just enough time to get there. Judging it a good moment, Roger moves into action: he leaps from the window and lunges towards Herbert. Alerted by the sound, the latter turns and immediately opens fire. The bullet narrowly misses Roger's head; he jumps up on his feet and swoops his enormous hand down on Herbert's head. The Nazi collapses and loses consciousness. Rolf has been watching the scene from afar. He starts up his snowbike and makes off at once.

'The bird is in our hands!' Roger announces to us over the radio.

John replies, just as feverishly:

'Perfect! Make sure no harm comes to him.'

Roger and Paul push the groggy Nazi into the cellar of the chalet and, after tying him up securely, inject him with a powerful sleeping draught. I land the helicopter near the chalet. John gets out, Roger takes his place and two minutes later, we launch into pursuit of Rolf, no longer concerned with concealing our presence. Meanwhile, Paul and John hurriedly retrieve the snowbikes that they had hidden at the edge of the riverbed.

A terrified Rolf throws hurried looks over his shoulder from time to time. He is not expecting the threat to come from ahead. Flying just over the ice, I make for him. Catching sight of the helicopter, the Nazi's eyes open wide. Astride his snowbike, he accelerates and makes straight for us, giving a terrified scream when the helicopter goes over his head with a deafening din.

I turn and go back to our prey. Rolf has stopped. He is waiting for us on his snowbike, unflinching, his rifle loaded and pointed in our direction. I make the helicopter shake, turning it right then left, preventing him from taking aim. A petrified Rolf falls from his snowbike; he then manages to fire off a volley of shots, but they all miss. Gripping his rifle, he gets back onto his vehicle, starts up in a furious hurry and sets off for the other side of the river. Several yards on, his snowbike slips and skids on the layer of ice. He almost loses balance, stops, seizes his rifle, points it at us again, and fires. But this time the weapon jams.

I head for him again. Rolf has regained control of his snowbike. He changes direction and veers off towards the opposite bank. The snowbike thrusts ahead, making impressive leaps, towards what seems an almost insurmountable obstacle. Defying the danger, Rolf does not alter the course on which his vehicle is heading, while Roger and I watch him incredulously:

'Is he mad?'

'No, he realises that if he gets back onto the bank, he has a chance of getting out.'

The snowbike reaches the obstacle at full speed. A slight slope allows him to take off – he lifts into the air, turns, then comes crashing down onto the ground. Under the impact of the shock, the thick layer of ice cracks in several places.

Dismayed, we watch the snowbike and Rolf disappearing into the depths of the river.

I bring the helicopter to a standstill above the hole in the ice. We scrutinise the dark waters that have been stirred up by the air from the propeller. Rolf is trying to swim. We see him sink then rise to the surface, gesticulating, before floundering again. We cannot let him drown without intervening. Our job is to capture him so that he can be tried. In any case, we do not want to leave traces behind us.

'Shit, we have to do something!'

'I'll take care of it,' says Roger.

In the back, he puts on his frogman suit, opens the door and gets hold of the rope hanging on the end of the winch. I slowly lower the rope while holding the helicopter steady. Rolf's chances of survival in the icy water are minimal and Roger knows he must act quickly. He dives in.

Less than two minutes later, he emerges holding the Nazi by the neck. It is too late: he has died from the cold. We cannot leave him there. The corpse is winched up then put into the cockpit of the helicopter. An hour later we bury him, not without difficulty, in the forest.

On the return journey, we pick up the equipment abandoned by Rolf. Roger inspects the Nazi's weapon before holding it out to me:

'We were lucky. The charger? Is jammed.'

Back at the chalet, we bring Herbert out of his cellar, wrapping him in a blanket and shoving him into the hold under the helicopter, with all the equipment that we had picked up on the ground. For us, Herbert is nothing more or less than a package that we have to deliver to the right destination.

We immediately take off again, flying over the places of our chase on our way. A last passage over the hole in the ice and we leave this place without looking back.

\*

We land carefully on the improvised heliport of our head-quarters on Orleans Island. Barney is waiting for us, burning with impatience. He clasps each one of us in his arms, congratulating and thanking us, then asks nervously:

'Do you have him with you? Where is he?'

I point to the hold under the helicopter.

Suddenly, Barney's attitude changes totally. He becomes distant, serious; his reserve betrays the enormous tension that is flooding over him.

'Take him inside.'

We untie Herbert, then push him unceremoniously into a room that has been transformed into an interrogation chamber, where Barney has already taken his place. Later, Roger, who was present at the interview, will tell me that he had not dared light a cigarette for fear that the whole house would explode, such was the electricity that was in the air at that moment...

Barney's behaviour is remarkable. He is face to face for the first time with one of the monsters who decimated his family and caused him so much suffering. One of the 'devil's envoys', as he calls them. One of those creatures whom he has vowed to pursue until he finally satisfies his vengeance. However, his calm and his apparent detachment during Herbert's extensive interrogation leave all the witnesses speechless with admiration. During the two days of interrogation, the Nazi will 'squeal' and denounce his acoloytes, selling them down the line. He will confess all his crimes and plead guilty to all the accusations laid against him, one after the other. The information he gives us will be precious to us during the final phase of the tracking and elimination of the Nazi cell. Barney plays the role of examining judge. He is a born interrogator. He is without equal in the skill with which he enmeshes his victim in a spider's web from which there can be no escape. At the end of the interrogation, he gathers us all together. Jane, who has come especially for the occasion, looks at her husband with tears in her eyes, while I have a lump in my throat and am unable to speak a word.

Herbert is brought into the room. It is a broken man who stands there facing us.

'We are here as witnesses to the victory of the Jewish people,' Barney declares to the prisoner. 'You others have become hunted, pathetic rats. Your fate is sealed.'

Then John puts a bag over Herbert's head and takes him out of the room. We will never see him again. John will accompany him to California to put him into the hands of the other branch of our organisation, responsible for organising the trial in which Herbert will have to answer for his responsibility for the death of tens of thousands of Jews, including thousands of children. We will never hear of him again.

## CHAPTER 13

# END GAME

THE BEGINNINGS OF SPRING ARE IN THE AIR, AWAKENING THE VAST FROZEN STRETCHES OF ALASKA. Nature is preparing to free itself from the terrible yoke of an endless winter. The melting of the ice and snow gives new life to the rivers that have been frozen and silent for many long months. Kodiak Island is among the first to emerge from hibernation. The Owl has made its nest not far from here, on a petrol rig belonging to one of Barney's companies, right in the heart of the Gulf of Alaska. We have captured a Nazi – but Dr Death is still at large. Our mission continues.

The old, isolated derrick is being repaired and the little team of workers who are mainly occupied with the renovation of the lower platform do not disturb us. For them, we are a team of ornithologists who have come to study the arrival of spring on the neighbouring island. The helicopter, which Barney has bought back in his petrol company's name, has all the necessary authorisation to cross American and Canadian airspace; an invaluable means of transport in this desolate region where everything happens through air and maritime connections. The voluminous equipment, brought from Orleans Island, has been stored on the upper deck, in a compartment reserved for us. That is where we gather. It is also from here that we will fly to track down the last Nazis who have taken refuge on Kodiak Island.

It is more than a month since the former SS men Gunther and Dino arrived in the town of Kodiak City; after having stocked up on provisions, they continued on westwards to Gunther's cabin, not far from the town of Karlak on the estuary of the river of the same name. Wild and magnificent, the region around the lake is filled with grizzly bears. The bears of Kodiak sow terror all around: beware to those who venture to violate their territory. And this is not the least of the challenges that nature has in store for us. The lake and its surroundings are infested with black flies, from which we suffer repeated attacks, in common with all the living creatures in the region.

The fog that continually covers Kodiak Island, particularly on the western side, in spring and summer, thwarts our plans. It is dangerous to go on foot into the forest because of the hungry bears who, at this time of the year, are waking from hibernation. On the other hand, kayaks and Zodiacs allow us to move around with complete discretion. No telephone line runs across the island; here, communication is only by radio.

Harry and Sharon, who has replaced Suzanne, have hired a small fishing boat. Anchored near Karluk, it seems to form part of the landscape, amid the flotilla of boats anchored in the port. Who could imagine that under the innocent appearance of a fishing boat is hidden a little spy vessel equipped with the most sophisticated electronic listening material? Who would think that the fishermen who had officially chartered it for their leisure activities are more interested in hunting for radiophonic signals and messages than fish or seafood?

Terrified, the Nazis are cloistered in their cabin in the middle of the forest. Only the wives, Roda and Sophie, risk going out occasionally, clinging on to each other's company and scared to split up. They go to do their shopping in Karluk, returning immediately to their hideout. During one of these outings to town, we observe them in a long discussion with the owner of a fishing boat. Are the group thinking of escaping once again? It will not take long for us to find out.

Just returned from California where he went to deliver Herbert to his judges, John assists us. Thanks to a frequency selector, he manages to intercept a conversation between the Nazis and a local air company that owns water planes that serve Kodiak Island. They discuss the possibility of taking two passengers to the airport in the capital, Anchorage, from the

Ugak Gulf, an enormous fjord that penetrates into the interior of the island like a tongue, from north to south.

The following day we intercept another conversation. The Nazis confirm the departure of the two women. They are no longer talking about going to Anchorage but to Vienna, The air company will take care of booking the various connections. Several days later, the two women arrive in the Austrian town of Abensee, about seventy miles from Salzburg, where they go to ground. Let them stay there – they do not interest us, unlike Gunther and Dino.

\*

In the Nazis' cabin, everything appears calm. The radio bug gives us nothing interesting. Do the two men believe themselves safe in this forest ruled by bears? Are they saying to themselves that in addition to the chronic fog, the grizzly bears represent the surest and most natural protection in the world? If they are, they are ignoring the determination of a much more dangerous predator: The Owl...

The winter is coming to an end and the spring is so short that we barely have time to take advantage of it. The days get longer and the hours of darkness decrease. In our plans, we have to take account of the wild character of the terrain and the dangers to which we expose ourselves in penetrating into bear country.

On board the platform, we put the finishing touches to our

last preparations: checking the arms and silencers, the capsules of tear gas to deter bears and any other unwelcome visitor, and the smoke bombs. We pile our equipment into the two-man kayaks, attached to landing buoys fixed to the feet of the helicopter, enabling it to land on lakes. The fateful hour is postponed several times, because of the thick fog covering the region of the fjord.

Taking advantage of a clearing in the fog, we decide to act and climb into the helicopter, which takes off from the platform, laden with material. We soon arrive above our destination. At the controls, I have trouble locating the spot. The breaks in the fog reveal the sky but not the ground. Only after my third circle in the air do I find, not without difficulty, a satisfactory landing site, near the sea, several miles from the planned spot.

Because of the state of the terrain around the cabin and the thickness of the forest, we have decided to land several miles from the Nazis' hideout. We have had to give up the idea of landing on the little lake, so as not to alert our prey with the sound of the engine. Not really having a choice, we have opted for the most distant and least comfortable solution, but it gives us the advantage of allowing us to approach without being discovered.

Paul, Roger, John and I slip outside the helicopter, untie the kayaks and put them in the water. Our many hours of training bear their fruit and we move off rapidly, moving to a good rhythm along the bank of the fjord, with its dense vegetation that comes right down to the water. Over a mile further on, we step onto dry land. Carrying our kayaks, we move along in complete silence, so as not to disturb the masters of these woods. Just in case, we have our weapons at the ready, with the silencers attached. The excitement mounts; at even the slightest unexpected noise, we jump and freeze for a moment. We go into a clearing. In the distance, at the edge of the woods, a group of bears are busy with their activities. We advance softly, risking at every second finding ourselves face to face with one of these furious beasts. The grizzlies have neither seen nor sensed us – not yet, anyway… The anxiety is palpable. My heart is beating wildly – unlike my comrades, who are Vietnam veterans, I have no experience of secret missions in the heart of forests… I look all around, nervously searching for any trace of danger. When we are far from the clearing, well sheltered in the foliage, we heave a sigh of relief.

An hour later, we finally get to the area of the cabin. We stop and, getting our breath, go over every detail of our plan. We take our positions, dispersing anti-bear products – of uncertain efficacy. We have now only to wait for dark to move to action.

Soon, it is pitch black. Infra-red glasses on our nose, we put our kayaks in the water in the still freezing lake and take our places. Careful not to make any noise, we stroke the water with our oars. The two kayaks advance slowly, one behind the other. The pale light of oil lamps, not far away, gives away the Nazis' house. The cabin is completely isolated, at the end of the world. They have no electricity, not even a generator. A small well dug in the back yard gives them the water they need.

Around 11 pm, the last lamp goes out, plunging the building into total darkness. We have difficulty repressing our desire to rush in and bring the operation to its conclusion. Crouching in the fog, we prefer to wait until the Nazis are asleep to act, for the surprise effect.

At midnight, at the signal, we split up into two platoons and slip silently towards the house. We are wearing firemen's gas masks. The first group positions themselves at the front door and the second in front of the exit that goes out onto the back yard. We break the windows with our rifle butts and throw three smoke bombs into the inside of the cabin. The smoke spreads quickly. For a moment, we fear that the sleeping Nazis will suffocate. We are about to force open the door when we hear Gunther and Dino shouting hysterically in German: 'Fire! Fire!' Then we hear fits of hoarse coughing and wild shouts. After a minute, the SS officers rush out and collapse in the yard.

They look pathetic and yet we feel no pity for them. Only our promise to bring them to justice prevents us from strangling these assassins. We immobilise them by tying them up. The two Nazis do not stop coughing. We hand them oxygen masks to help them breathe.

'Who are you? What do you want?' asks Gunther, terrified and exhausted.

The two men are trembling.

'If you do what we tell you, we will not harm you,' John replies in excellent German in an authorative tone that leaves no doubt as to the seriousness of their situation.

The two Nazis content themselves with nodding their heads. We take them back inside the cabin before tying them to each other.

'You are not permitted to talk,' John orders.

In the cabin, there is almost no smoke left; Paul and John are searching the place meticulously. Finding nothing, John goes back to see the two prisoners:

'Where is it?'

'What are you talking about?'

'You know perfectly well. We haven't found anything – no papers, no money. Nothing. So they must be hidden. I am asking you a last time: where is your safe?'

John is looking at the two men with a mocking, vaguely threatening, air. One of them replies:

'In the room next door, under the rug. A little safe, under a floorboard. I will give you the combination.'

The contents of the first shelf of the safe does not surprise us - here is all the paraphernalia of the fugitive. A waterproof holder, hidden in the false-bottomed lid, contains documents and interesting notes about 'treasure' hidden in lakes in Switzerland and Austria. Here we read the familiar names of Klunteler and Traunsee, which we have already come across in the documents found in Aribert Heim's briefcase after the Seven Lakes mission.

# END GAME

Interrogated by John, Dino describes in detail the content of the chests. He says that he personally took part in loading them with treasure, describes the colour of the waterproof bags into which the booty was wrapped and reveals to us the exact number of lead boxes that were deposited on the bottom of the lake. This information corroborates what we know already. Some of us are now envisaging mounting an operation to recuperate the Nazis' treasure. But that is another story...

\*

I leave the chalet with Roger at dawn. We are halfway up the slope of a hill, when an enormous grizzly, who is apparently very angry, comes out of the forest without warning and rushes towards us. Panicking, we take refuge in a tree. We do not want to open fire, hoping the bear will calm down and leave us alone. We throw a smoke bomb in his direction and the smoke stops him, making him take several steps back. A second bomb unleashes his fury. Perched up on his hind legs, he strikes a resolutely hostile attitude and begins growling, his mouth wide open. Then he turns round and goes back into the forest, in the middle of a thick cloud of smoke. The silence around does not augur well: it is the lull before the storm.

Once the smoke has cleared, we remain at the top of the tree, fearing that the beast will return.

'I'd be surprised if the grizzly gave up so easily,' says Roger, coming down from the tree. 'Let's get out of here quick.'

We start running, a tight knot of fear in our stomachs, then stop, ten minutes later, to load our weapons: we have heard noises in the thickets. The shrubs move, then there is the sound of growling, and the grizzly stands facing us once again. Suddenly, he makes for us.

'Shit!' screams Roger, firing at the bear, wounding him in the stomach and halting his charge.

Calmly, I aim at the bear's head and shoot. The wild animal collapses with all his weight onto the ground. Roger gives him the coup de grâce. Then we move off, without a word. I know that both of us are thinking the same thing: this wild beast is not the last one that we have to defeat...

Half an hour later, we reach the helicopter. I settle myself at the controls of the machine, which rises into the air and heads for the cabin to proceed to evacuate the whole company. Roger has remained on the ground to prepare for our departure by sea. Meanwhile, Sharon and Harry, remaining on board our 'fishing boat' make for the little creek from where the evacuation of the Nazis will begin.

Landing on the edge of the little lake, near the cabin, I catch sight of the two Nazis. They are no longer tied together but laid on the ground, immobile, under the influence of the drug with which they have been injected, covered with old military blankets found in their hideout.

We load them, dozily leaning against each other, into the copter and attach them to their seats. Paul sits beside them to make sure that nothing goes wrong during the flight.

# END GAME

After having got rid of every trace likely to lead to the identification of the owners, John gives me the green light to lift off. Ten minutes later, I land the machine on the bank of the gulf. The Nazis are taken away in the inflatable dinghy to the fishing boat, which is preparing to make its unhurried way to the north. From up high, I see it disappearing into the fog of Ugak fjord.

\*

Bit by bit, we have succeeded in eliminating the Nazi cell we have been pursuing for so many long months. Only one now remains. He is alone, isolated, unwell. We know where he is and how to reach him. It is our last appointment with Dr Death.

# CHAPTER 14

# IN THE CLAWS
# OF THE OWL

ARIBERT HEIM HAS BEEN TAKEN TO ONE OF THE BIGGEST
HOSPITALS IN QUEBEC, PLACED IN TOTAL ISOLATION AND
UNDER VERY STRICT SURVEILLANCE IN A PROTECTED WING OF
THE BUILDING. Our colleagues have not managed to get any
information about his condition. Jane tries to get something
from her highly placed contacts within Quebecker medical
circles, but in vain. The same fiasco occurs for Gerald, whose
investigative talents come up against a real conspiracy of
silence: he does not manage to extract the slightest wisp of
information from the hospital's medical staff.

Are the staff indeed effectively ignorant of everything that
happens in that special, isolated wing of the hospital where the
Nazi is cared for? Are they forced to divulge nothing of this

mysterious patient who has doubtless been entered under a false name?

The Nazis have obviously benefited from wide-ranging external support. We will need to use ruses and initiative to get the information we need. But luck – or destiny, perhaps - is on our side. From having hung around the surroundings of the hospital, Gerald eventually makes the acquaintance of a member of the sanitary staff who works on the floor just above the one where the rat is hospitalised. He has just come back to his post after a long sick leave.

Gerald introduces himself to his new friend as the editor of an international medical review and proposes that he take part in a report that will be published throughout the world. The man, who is sympathetic and open, is enthusiastic about the idea of seeing his name associated with a report that will appear in a prestigious medical review; Gerald is carefully weaving his web.

Meanwhile, the entire team of The Owl has gathered. Now that the fate of Heim's Nazi accomplices is sealed, we can all concentrate together on our last mission. We learn that Berti, Elsa and the unidentified 'three musketeers' who helped our prey flee to Canada take turns at Heim's bedside.

The contacts between Gerald and the local sanitary worker are more and more frequent. Gerald photographs his friend in uniform against the outside of the hospital, then conducts a long interview with him about his work. To recompense him for his efforts, he gives him a considerable sum of money, to which our 'unwitting spy' is not indifferent – he is ready to do anything to deserve it. All his meetings with Gerald are filmed. The worker's trust grows day by day and the information starts coming: he reveals practically all the secrets of the hospital and boasts of having unlimited access to every corner and every department of the hospital. Gerald decides to put him to the test; saying to him in a haughty tone:

'All the same, things happen in the hospital that you don't know about...'

Our poor accomplice falls right into the trap:

'If you are insinuating that something shady is going on on the floor above, I can tell you it is a member of the New York Italian mafia and very soon I'll be able to prove that I'm telling the truth.'

He takes Gerald's comment absolutely seriously and after several hours, the team receives Heim's complete medical file. That is how we learn that the doctors have given an 'encouraging' prognosis: the Nazi's general condition has greatly improved.

The sanitary worker is an intelligent, capable man. Soon realising that he is dealing with a rather unusual journalist, he joins in the game and agrees to help Gerald, whom he perhaps takes for a Canadian police officer or a member of the FBI charged with spying on the mysterious, isolated godfather on the top floor of the hospital... Thanks to him, the organisation manages to introduce two small listening devices near the rat, one in his room and the second in a small adjoining room, where a nurse-bodyguard is found most of the time. From now on, the members of the team are able to listen secretly to all the Nazis' conversations and can form a precise idea of their programme.

Berti, Elsa and their accomplices take it in turns to watch over Aribert Heim, following the timetables with very Germanic rigidity and thereby making our task all the easier. The gang are staying near the hotel, in a house belonging to one of the 'three musketeers', a professional man whose father was an emigrant Nazi who took refuge in Canada; unable to obtain official leave to remain, the Nazi disappeared into the north of the country. His two other companions also belong to the second generation of Nazis; they are too young to have known the Third Reich for which they are nostalgic. Both possess American passports.

For us, the 'three musketeers' represent no danger. True, they belong to a formidable Nazi cell but their capacity to harm is limited to several sporadic anti-Semitic activities, above all to giving our prey logistic support. Unlike Berti and Elsa, who are out-and-out SS, we do not take them very seriously. However, we decide to get them out of the game. Gerald takes care of the intimidation tactics. After having found in his mailbox an anonymous message accusing him of belonging to a secret organisation that endangers Canadian democracy and threatening to reveal his activity to the local security services, one of them abruptly disappears. We later learn that he has gone back to the United States. We will hear no more about him.

Thanks to the information gleaned from the sanitary

service worker, we develop a plan of action – without this increasingly valuable data, we would never have been able to draw it up. For hours, we pore over maps of the hospital. We study the electrical installations, dissect the network of pipes, probe the air conditioning and ventilation systems and examine the labyrinth of double ceilings. Finally, we take a decision – our new mission is to take the Nazi from his room, while he is asleep.

*

It is after midnight. The ambulance we have procured drives into the precincts of the hospital. I am at the steering wheel. Gerald holds out to the security guard the official papers, duly stamped, that authorise our presence. We have come to transfer a patient. We omit only to specify that it is Aribert Heim... We park the vehicle in the basement, not far from the entrance. The place is deserted; the hospital is asleep. Wearing our white overalls, stethoscopes around our neck, doctors' bags in our hands, we enter one of the lifts and go up to the top floor, where the Nazi is installed.

The door opens onto a deserted, silent corridor. Here, no need of a reception desk. We make towards the left wing. A heavy, barred door blocks the corridor (Gerald had procured the keys of all the doors in the hospital – I will not say how here, so as not to harm anyone). The key turns in the lock but the door does not open; it is blocked on the other side by thick bars. We were expecting this. Gerald gives me a leg-up and I reach the double ceiling which I lift and put aside before hoisting up my comrade. Twenty seconds later, we are on the other side of the door and making silently for the room where the bodyguard, Dr Death's guardian angel, is sleeping. When we get to the half-open door, we pause a moment. All is calm. I throw a rapid glance around the room. The guard is asleep in a chair, his head leaning back. His breathing is not regular; he is only in a light sleep.

We get the gas masks out of our bags and put them on. Roger takes a cartridge of sleeping gas, activates it and places it at the entrance to the room. Soon, the guard's breathing gets heavier. We wait another few minutes before going into the room to reassure ourselves that the man is in deep sleep. I search him and confiscate a Colt 45 — far too powerful a weapon, given their needs and above all the place where he is... Moving out of the room, we hear more deep breathing coming from the neighbouring room: that of Aribert Heim, who has also been affected by the gas.

Roger takes his pulse. Everything is fine. He has a bandage on his shoulder and another on his leg — where we hit him during the shoot-out at the lake. I contemplate our prey's face. It is that of a tired old man. I feel at a loss. This moment is supposed to be the most overwhelming and stupefying of all these long months, the completion of the whole operation. My heart should be jumping for joy. Instead of which, I have a gnawing feeling inside. I feel something that resembles huge disappointment. After all the efforts we have expended to arrive at this moment, I find it hard to explain to myself the reason for this confusion. The final act of the operation, the capture of enemy number one, the head of the Nazi cell, has been reduced to a technical episode. The spectacle of this pathetic Nazi is so wretched that I have trouble believing that this unworthy, impotent being is the monster responsible for so many murders and atrocities in Mauthausen camp. Suddenly, the desire for vengeance that has been driving me for years gives way to disgust mingled with horror.

Aribert Heim moves. He seems to want to wake up. Opens an eye. Has he seen us? He immediately plunges back into sleep. Roger gets a syringe out of his bag, fills it with a powerful sedative that he injects into the Nazi's drip. We are now sure that he will not wake up. Stretched out on the bed, inert, he is completely cut off from the land of the living. I leave the room, open the grille and then, with the help of a masterkey, open the door of a store room not far away; I get out the wheeled bin that is inside and return to the room.

After having removed his drip, we seize Heim and bundle him unceremoniously into the large rubbish bin, then gather our personal belongings which we throw on top of him, covering it all with his sheets. We carefully remove any trace of our presence, picking up the gas capsule which we also throw into the bin. We leave in an obvious place a letter explaining the reasons for the disappearance of Aribert Heim. Signed in the name of a spectral Nazi organisation, it contains precise instructions for the rat's friends, enjoining them to say nothing and to disappear as quickly as possible, because of the danger threatening them. This is a delicate reference aimed at Berti and Elsa, designed to terrify them a bit more. When they find the letter, Dr Death will already be on his way to meet his destiny.

We take the wheeled bin into the service lift and go down to the basement, where Roger and Paul are waiting for us in the vehicle that is going to get us out of the hospital. The Nazi, who is sleeping deeply, is pushed into the car and we set off, driving slowly so as not to attract attention.

As soon as we have left the car park, we alert Barney:

'We have the rat.'

Over the radio, a cry of joy rings out. Then there is silence, a heavy silence. I could swear that I hear Barney stifling a sob.

'We will meet as agreed,' he says, before ending the communication.

We had initially planned to take the Nazi to Orleans Island, but have given up that idea, for security reasons; we do not know how Aribert Heim's men will react. It is likely they will attempt to pursue us. We have therefore decided to send him at once to his final destination.

Half an hour later, our car stops in the middle of some wasteland outside the city of Quebec, in front of our caravan. The members of The Owl, in their entirety, give us a hero's welcome. In the hugs they give us, our friends express all the tension accumulated over the course of these months of exhausting tracking. Our nerves are still on edge, but eventually this is dissipated by emotion. I will never forget Jane's eyes brimming with tears, Barney's trembling or our comrades' display of affection.

We open the boot of the car. Under a heap of dirty linen, stained sheets and creased clothes, we make out a human form. It is hard to believe. The sleeping body we are looking at is that of one of the greatest criminals of the century, a monster who has pride of place in the pantheon of torturers, in the foremost pack of the most wanted Nazis on the planet, just behind Joseph Mengele and Aloïs Brunner.

'He's asleep.'

'When he wakes up, he will confront his judges.'

Contemplating the rat, I have only a single regret: that we cannot announce his capture to the whole world. I know that we will have to keep people and history ignorant of it for a long time. That is the price to pay for our revenge: we must remain in the shadows. And that is why the most incriminating details of this story will remain forever secret.

Barney comes forward in his turn. Transfigured. He has lost his air of an American millionaire. We see in him the terrified little boy, deported to Mauthausen when Aribert Heim was practising there. Tears in his eyes, he utters a single phrase, in a voice that is practically soundless:

'At last!'

# EPILOGUE

A MONTH HAS PASSED SINCE ARIBERT HEIM'S CAPTURE. OUR PRINCIPAL MISSION HAS BEEN ACCOMPLISHED. Almost half of the members of The Owl have left us. They have played more than their part; they will immediately assume anonymity again and disappear to the four corners of the United States, without leaving any traces.

This ending is painful, almost shocking. But that is how it is and we can do nothing about it: separation was written into the genes of The Owl. When he took each of us on, Barney had clearly specified that once the mission was over, we would never see each other again. We had therefore taken our leave of some of our friends after having lifted our champagne glasses, to our health and to the memory of the children of the Holocaust.

That is how the activities of The Owl on the eastern coast of North America ends. It is the end of a period of long hours of sacrifice and perseverance, in often extreme, testing conditions. The house on Orleans Island is still at our disposal and will be for several months to come, before being restored to its owner, but the operational equipment, including the helicopter, has been evacuated and transported to the west, onto Barney's oil platform in the sea off Kodiak Island, in the gulf of Alaska.

*

It remains for me to explain what happened to the rat.

After having been 'introduced' to Aribert Heim, Barney and Jane left for California to prepare the trial, the last act in our play. Roger checked the condition of Dr Death, still stretched out in the boot of our monospace, while I got behind the steering wheel with Paul at my side. Our destination: the isolated heliport where our Bell 206 was waiting for us. Once the rat was loaded into the helicopter, we headed due south, to a private airport belonging to one of Barney's oil companies.

The transfer of Aribert Heim to his final destination had been meticulously prepared. Nothing had been left to chance. No sooner had we landed than four men surrounded the helicopter and loaded the Nazi on board a little two-engined 'Chieftain'. The rat was still half asleep.

During the flight I went to check regularly on our prey. He

was now in a light sleep and moving around… Leaning over him to sit him up, I noticed that he was wearing a chain around his neck. I inspected it more closely – it was an Iron Cross. Blood rose to my head and I lost my self-control. Suddenly, Heim opened his eyes. I screamed:

'How did you get that cross? By killing thousands of Jews, wasn't it?'

Dr Death did not reply. He closed his eyes once again; I didn't know whether he was still asleep or terrified.

I felt murderous rage.

'Calm down,' said Roger.

Mad with anger, I tore off the Iron Cross and went to sit down again. One of our team buckled the rat's belt while another injected him once more with a light sedative.

I have often wondered why one of the most wanted Nazis on the planet had walked around for years with an Iron Cross around his neck. To answer that question, one must remember that Aribert Heim lived in Baden-Baden for almost twenty years, under his real name, that his house still bears his plaque and that even while in hiding he continued to be officially responsible for his property affairs in Berlin. This was a man who experienced no fear, shame or doubt.

Before our final destination, we made two stops. The first to refuel and to 'pack' our cumbersome passenger. As soon as the engines of the plane stopped reverberating on the deserted runway of a small private aerodrome in the centre of the United States, the 'cleaning' team climbed aboard. From that point, everything happened according to a script that had been meticulously written in advance. Heim was installed in a box that had been made to his measurements. One of the 'cleaners' had given him an oxygen mask and taken his pulse before closing the lid again. Then the box was carefully slipped into the baggage hold. Our second stop was at Van Nuys airport in Los Angeles, the biggest private airport in the world. Firstly to fill up again on fuel but above all to take on board another passenger — one of the leaders of the organisation, who had also survived the Holocaust, and whose name I will keep secret for security reasons. Once on board, our twin-engined plane took off and made for the west. Soon, we were flying over the ocean.

Night fell. The last stage of our journey was over.

\*

Catalina, a little, rocky island situated twenty or so miles from the Californian coast, is the only island in the region to be permanently inhabited. Its some 30,000 souls live in the town of Avalon. The rest of the island is a natural park. For centuries, because of its geographical situation, Catalina has served as an operational base for all sorts of smugglers, pirates, privateers and other adventurers of the seas. But it was another kind of privateer who besieged it that evening in spring 1982.

It was almost night when our plane flew over the northern tip of the island and made for the runways of the local airport.

# EPILOGUE

We had carefully chosen our time of arrival. There was little chance that we would run into someone around the landing zone. On the spot, our welcoming party confirmed to us over the radio that we could land without risk of being seen. Once the plane was stationary, colleagues from the Californian branch of The Owl seized the box in which Aribert Heim was sleeping. They loaded it onto one of the few vehicles authorised to drive on the island, before disappearing into the night.

Since then, no one has seen Aribert Heim alive. I knew that he was judged by a special court several days later. Found guilty of the assassination of thousands of Jews and dozens of Spanish resistance fighters deported to Mauthausen, Dr Death was executed. I do not know where he was buried, if he was buried. What do I care about the site of his grave, as long as no one can ever go and stand there in remembrance?

For me, the story was not over. I saw Barney again several times, during a reception organised in honour of our team in a luxurious executive apartment in one of his buildings on Central Park in New York. The only members of the team to have already gone there, John and Harry had nicknamed it 'Ali Barney's cave'. The place had more the air of a museum than of someone's home. Refreshments were served to us in our room groaning with Greek and Roman antiquities, arranged with impeccable taste. One wing of this castle-apartment was dedicated to the memory of Barney and Jane's family, friends and loved ones. All massacred during the Holocaust. At the end of this little memorial, on the ceiling of a large room decorated

247

in dark mahogany, a gigantic chandelier in the form of a tree with its roots growing upwards has pride of place. The brilliance of the light reflecting on six million crystals shaped like hearts suspended on the branches filled the room with radiance. On the eastern wall, in the direction of Jerusalem, was inscribed in golden letters: 'The people of God will never perish, for their roots are planted in celestial spheres.' Tears in my eyes, I contemplated this symbol of the hope of the Jewish people and their eternal existence, forged in blood and suffering. We could not imagine a more fitting final accolade to our operation. The memory of the massacred children had been our compass and the memory of the six million victims our burning protection – our wall of fire. I remember that painful proverb: 'Against the avenging of a child's death, the Devil himself is powerless.'

At the end of this reunion, Barney took John, Roger, Paul and me aside. Thanks to the information gathered during this long tracking, we would be able to attack the international branches of Aribert Heim's organisation. The Californian group had already begun. Some of their men were now to be found in Caracas in Venezuela, where other war criminals had gone to ground. And then, we would have to think seriously about mounting an expedition to recuperate the Nazi treasure buried in the Swiss and Austrian lakes – but that, as I have said, is another story...

# WHAT HAPPENED
# TO THEM?

I STAYED IN CONTACT WITH ROGER. WE BOTH LATER MET UP AGAIN WITH JOHN. All three of us decided to investigate the story of the 'lost treasure' of the lakes of Toplitz, Klunteler and Traunsee in Austria. The operation bore the name of 'Seals' treasure' – and that is all that I can say about it today…

Sean, Harry, Gerald, Sharon, Paul and Suzanne disappeared to the United States. I have never heard of them again.

John and Roger are the only ones never to have lost contact with Jane and Barney. For my part, I met up with Barney again ten years after our adventure.

Elsa and Berti never went back to the little town of St Joachim in Canada. Their house was sold by a local estate agency and the money of the sale transferred to a bank account in Austria.

The trail of Roda and Sophie, the wives of Gunther and Dino, ran out in Austria and we never tried to track them down.

Karl and Monika sold their house in Quebec and settled in a smart suburb of Caracas in Venezuela.

We were never able to track down the medical assistants who took it in turns to visit Aribert Heim in his sick bed.

The Owl put an end to its activities shortly after the elimination of Aribert Heim's entire cell. According to false information, an alarm was sounded while we were in Latin America. The members of the team dispersed to the four corners of the globe. The reasons for the false alarm were never brought to light.

The Owl captured a dozen Nazi criminals, who were all judged and subsequently executed.